Probably Benign

A devastating diagnosis, a 500 mile journey, & a quest to advance the next generation of breast cancer screening

So *More* Women with Breast Cancer Become *Survivors*

Leslie Ferris Yerger
with Stephen Copeland

CORE.

Probably Benign
A Devastating Diagnosis, a 500-Mile Journey, and a Quest to Advance the Next
Generation of Breast Cancer Screening
www.probablybenign.com

Published by The Core Media Group, Inc.
P.O. Box 2037, Indian Trail, NC 28079
www.thecoremediagroup.com

Cover & Interior Design: Nadia Guy

ISBN 978-1-950465-25-5

Unless otherwise indicated, scripture quotations in this book are taken from the *The
Holy Bible, New International Version*®, *NIV*®, Copyright © 1973, 1978, 1984, 2011
by Biblica, Inc.® Used by permission. All rights reserved worldwide.

This book is for information purposes only and is not a substitute for medical advice
from a physician. Please see your doctor for medical care, questions, concerns, or a
diagnosis.

Printed in the United States of America.

Table of Contents

Note to the Reader

Dear women everywhere or anybody who loves one:

To be sure, I am not famous or a member of the media or a Hollywood star, nor am I particularly rich. That makes me pretty much just like most of you. In fact, I *could* be you—your daughter, your mother, your sister, your friend, or your coworker. I could be any woman you've ever loved in any way, for any reason. So in that way, I am nobody in particular, but rather I am anybody. In that sense, I am also everybody.

And that's precisely the problem.

The fact that what happened to me really could happen to you and to anybody you know is exactly why I wrote this book. This book, then, is not really about me and my journey, but more about you and yours. Through my story of diagnosis and walking the Camino de Santiago, I hope you will learn something about yourself, your own breast density, your own approach (or your loved ones' approach) to breast cancer screening, your life, and how to unleash what resides in your heart.

I also hope you will feel empowered to get additional breast cancer screening, should that be what you deem you want for yourself, no matter what it takes. I hope you'll feel empowered to take ownership over your own body and your own life and no longer let others or the systems at play in this world control what is already yours.

And finally, I hope you will share this book and the messages inside with a friend or loved one so that one day, more breast cancers will be found earlier, when the chances of survival are greatest. So that ultimately *more* women with breast cancer become *survivors*.

Much love to all,
Leslie Ferris Yerger

A Word About the Title

"Do the best you can until you know better.
Then once you know better, do better."
-Maya Angelou

The title of this book is meant to grab your attention, to intrigue you enough to make you pick up the book and want to read a bit further, at least. Because you are reading this now, it may have just done its job!

As you may or may not know, the Breast Imaging Reporting and Data System (BI-RADS) is a numerical scale between 0 and 6, and "probably benign" is wording used when a mammogram reading is classified as Bi-RADS 3.[1] This is the category that says there might be something in the breast that could be cancerous but most likely isn't, hence the words *"probably benign."*

My goal here is not to quarrel with the BI-RADS scoring system or its wording. Nor is it to call into question what any doctor or patient does or doesn't do with a mammogram report that reads "probably benign."

Rather, I think it's a phrase that in many ways summarizes quite well the state of affairs with mammography in general. It tells the story

---

1. For more information about BI-RADS, see "Understanding Your Mammogram Report," cancer. org, https://www.cancer.org/cancer/breast-cancer/screening-tests-and-early-detection/mammograms/understanding-your-mammogram-report.html.

that often plays itself out when something is seen on a mammogram but is unclear whether it's benign or not. The result, sadly, is a guessing game—playing the odds about what it really is, since we don't know for sure, and the mammogram can't really tell us. We've all heard about these cases. Perhaps you know someone who has been told, "We think it's likely a cyst, so let's watch that spot and see if it grows." Another translation: "We think it's most likely not cancer, so we are going to check it again in a few months." To be fair, sometimes biopsies are taken when this BI-RADS rating is given, and many come back negative—thank goodness!

"There are more accurate ways to screen for breast cancer that give women the confidence they deserve. If healthcare providers would use these more accurate methods, far fewer women would have to hear the words 'probably benign' or would have to 'wait to see what happens.' And most importantly, fewer cancers would go completely undetected."

Even scarier, when a woman gets an "all clear" BI-RADS 1 rating, there still may be cancer there that is completely masked by dense breast tissue. That happens more than you might think, and that is extremely worrisome. There are more accurate ways to screen for breast cancer that give women the confidence they deserve. If healthcare providers would use these more accurate methods, far fewer women would have to hear the words "probably benign" or would have to "wait to see what happens." And most importantly, fewer cancers would go completely undetected.

"Probably benign" is quite an unsettling phrase, is it not? My goal in writing this book is to nudge us closer to a world where we can confidently and clearly say "benign" or "malignant." As technologically advanced as we are, everyone deserves a straightforward "yes" or "no." No more vague "probably" assessments…and a lot fewer instances in which breast cancer goes completely unseen because it is masked by dense breast tissue. Nothing is perfect, but there are ways to move closer toward perfection. That is part of what I hope to accomplish with this book.

We can do better, and if we can, then we must.

"Probably benign" and existing breast cancers that go unseen aren't good enough for anybody. Not for me. Not for you. However, the world of "maybe" or "not sure" or "let's watch that spot" or "it's probably just a cyst" is what we have come to accept as the norm. Why should we accept that these assessments are "just the way it is" when we can do better? We absolutely can do better, and I believe it starts with us refusing to accept the status quo.

- 1 -
Beginning Again

*"Your present circumstances don't determine where you can go.
They merely determine where you start."*
-Nido Qubein

A quick kiss good-bye, and then I turned and walked away, into
the unknown, to begin a journey, having no idea how or when
it would end.

As I left my husband in Saint-Jean-Pied-de-Port, France, following
The Frances Way of the Camino de Santiago, I found myself eager and
excited, yet a little leery for the journey ahead. I was not at all sure how
it was going to go, but I was determined to give it my best shot.

Never before had I attempted anything even close to spending four
to six weeks hiking alone. As a mother of three, never before had I had
the time to even consider attempting such a feat, nor would I have ever
indulged myself the time and space to do such a thing. But life was
different now, and my priorities had changed.

I got my first taste of the Camino de Santiago several months earlier,
when my husband and I took a trip to Portugal and Spain for our thirtieth wedding anniversary. One day, we hiked twelve miles into Santiago, and I got the idea that perhaps sometime I would try to hike the
entire five-hundred-mile Camino Frances route to Santiago by myself.
In some ways, it was an absurd thought. All we had done, after all, was

hike a dozen miles to a winery for an afternoon of wine tasting. That is nothing close to walking fifteen to seventeen miles on unpredictable terrain, day after day after day, for longer than a month in all weather conditions. But I had grown confident that I could do it. And more than that, I felt *called* to it somehow.

Sometimes there are notions like this that are hard to explain. Walking the Camino was one of those for me. If you ask other pilgrims (those who walk the Camino de Santiago), they will likely tell you that they weren't exactly sure why they started walking the Camino, but by the time they completed the journey, they had come to understand it.

Some of my family and friends were confused as to why I felt such a conviction to hike the Camino alone. I'm not even sure if my husband fully understood why I was determined to go solo. In our thirty years of marriage, we probably hadn't spent any more than a week apart from one another. Honestly, I probably didn't explain my reasons very well. But there is wisdom in Rumi's quote, "It's your road, and yours alone. Others may walk it with you, but no one can walk it for you." And this much I knew to be true.

I now see that the events that unfolded in my life led me to the foot of the Camino. Traumatic life events can change you. And they had certainly changed me. Strangely, they open you up to things you might not have done before. They can help you see life more clearly and hear the voices that are calling out to you. As people who have hiked the Camino will tell you, the path seeks you out and pulls you in. Though some hike the Camino with others, the majority of people do it alone. They decide to walk the road that no one can walk for them.

El Camino de Santiago

You can start the Camino just about anywhere. I met a couple who walked out of their back door in Switzerland and hiked the Camino for four months. Another pilgrim had been hiking for six months from Krakow, Poland, in honor of his best friend, who had died of cancer.

But the most well-known and well-marked routes are the seven in Spain. And the most popular of those, attracting more than two hundred thousand pilgrims a year, is the Camino Frances (The French Way), which stretches across the northern part of Spain, beginning just over the border into France and winding its way west five hundred miles toward the northwest coast of Spain, ending at the famous Cathedral at Santiago de Compostela in Galicia. You may have heard of this path through the movie *The Way*, starring Martin Sheen, which popularized the Camino in the States. The Camino Frances is the route I chose for my journey.

El Camino de Santiago means "the way" or "the route" or "the path to, or of, Saint James." James, Spain's patron saint, was an apostle and cousin of Jesus. As is detailed in the book of Acts in the New Testament, after Jesus's crucifixion and resurrection, all the apostles scattered to preach the Gospel. James went to the Iberian Peninsula, which is now Spain and Portugal. Upon returning home, he was beheaded by order of King Herod. It is said that James's followers took his body back to the Galicia area, to Santiago de Compostela. Today there is a shrine where James's bones are said to be kept in the Cathedral at Santiago de Compostela—where all paths of the Camino lead—attracting pilgrims since around 900 AD from all over the world. James is also the patron saint of pilgrims.

Memorials of James, depicted as a religious scholar with a book, a staff, and a scallop shell, are everywhere on the Camino—in town squares, in the cathedrals, and on the path itself. But "Santiago" is more than just the Spanish name for Saint James. It is a symbol. Not everyone who hikes the Camino is a Christian, but each person is a pilgrim.

No matter what you believe, I think that most find there's something inspiring about someone like James, who was true to his convictions and bold enough to give his life for a cause he believed in…something he hoped would change the world…something he hoped would move humanity forward in love and equality…something that stirred him within and gave birth to action. I guess you could say I stepped foot on the Camino looking for something that Saint James had found.

The Catalyst

A year before I began hiking the Camino, I had just turned fifty-five and had gone in for a mammogram and other standard health tests. It was also recommended that I get a baseline bone-density scan to compare against for bone loss as I got older. Shortly after I got the "all good, see you next year" call regarding my mammogram and ultrasound, I received a more mysterious call from the doctor. He said, "We see something strange in your hip, and we'd like for you to get an X-ray."

Not thinking too much of it, I promptly scheduled the X-ray

appointment. I did begin to get the idea that there might be something really wrong when the X-ray technician so sweetly asked me, "Does it hurt?"

"Does what hurt?" I responded. It was at that point when it struck me that there might be something really wrong, but of course I had no idea what it could be. I was not experiencing pain; my hip felt just fine. It was all very strange.

Quickly realizing I had no clue, she ran back into her equipment room and yelled to me, "You can go now; the doctor will call you!" I was slightly amused about that, but I would not have thought it comical at all had I had any notion of what was to come.

Several days later, I received a call from the doctor, who said to me, "You've got something really bad going on in your bones. It looks like multiple myeloma (bone cancer). This is more important than anything else you have going on. You need to see an oncologist ASAP."

Within the week, I was sitting at my oncologist's office, getting multiple tests. Two were for multiple myeloma, and both turned out to be negative. This was the agonizing part: the waiting...the phone tag... the lost sleep...all the while anticipating the worst.

During those endless weeks, I was grateful for those who were with me every step of the way between the phone calls, test results, and what felt like eternal waiting and wondering.

Every test came back negative. So what was it, then?

Either a benign bone disease or a cancer metastasis of some sort, according to my oncologist. A bone biopsy would tell the tale, and one was scheduled promptly. This entailed more appointment scheduling... waiting...phone tag...the procedure...and waiting about another week, all to wind up right back in the oncologist's office.

The dreaded diagnosis?

Stage 4 estrogen responsive lobular breast cancer.

But how? The diagnosis had come two months after a "clear" mammogram and ultrasound. I felt that surely there must be some mistake.

But, How Can It Be?

"But I just got a clear mammogram and an ultrasound," I said, shocked.

"Well, sometimes it can be very small and yet metastasize," my doctor explained.

What I had, however, was the exact opposite of small.

Imagine my confusion, dismay, shock, disbelief.

Given how it all went down, we decided a second opinion was in order.

Through my husband's work, we were able to engage with the Healthnetwork Foundation, an organization that helps people quickly find the best healthcare in the nation considering their location, specific medical problem, and personal preferences. What a relief it was to get help from Laura there, to quickly assess MD Anderson in Texas, Sloan Kettering in New York, Johns Hopkins in Baltimore, the University of Chicago, and Mayo Clinic in Minnesota. I decided that, along with Mayo being only five hours away from the suburbs of Chicago where I live, I also liked how Mayo looked, felt, and operated. Like the Camino, I felt something in my gut about that place. I believe that we as humans have a gut for a reason.

I realized very quickly upon arriving at the Mayo Clinic that I was in the right place. Though they treat thousands of people every day, when you are with them, you feel like you are the only one.

I asked my doctor there, "How can it be that two months ago I had a mammogram and an ultrasound, and everything was fine?"

He turned and said very matter-of-factly, "For women with dense breast tissue, a mammogram is like shining light through concrete… there are great limitations." To be sure, I was stunned by his response. I had *never* heard anything about this fact before in my life.

This was the very statement that prompted me to study, research, and try to understand exactly what he meant by it. It would be the impetus of my journey to help other women, so that my story doesn't become their story.

Two Unsettling Words

While getting an appointment at the Mayo Clinic, I had also retrieved the paperwork from my doctor detailing all my past mammogram reports and images. Most doctors don't give you these unless you ask for them. Honestly, I didn't know to ask. Well, as stress-invoking as a mammogram can be—with all the callbacks, all the time that elapses between phone calls, and all the cryptic evaluations—I was quite content with simply receiving a message from my doctor, letting me know that I was in the clear, as most women are.

In these papers, however, were my first encounter with the words "probably benign." Many years ago, I had been called back, as many women are, for "more pictures" because "we might see something, but we aren't sure." The words "probably benign" were used in that scenario. There is no way to know if that instance is related to what I have now, but seeing those two words used in a past report was alarming.

> "All I'm saying is that had it not been for my cancer diagnosis, I would not have felt the urgency to do what I knew I needed to do: follow the voice that was calling to me so that I could figure out exactly how I wanted the rest of my life to be—how I wanted to live it, say it, and be it. So that I could, like Saint James, live with a boldness and conviction in whatever time I have left in life."

In whose life is "probably benign" good enough?

Yet these words are in many mammogram reports.

If you had a gas leak in your house and your technician told you it was "probably fixed," you'd be livid. If you bought a set of tires and the seller said, "These tires will probably get you where you want to go," would you go ahead and buy them? And would you be happy with paying for an inspection of your house that finds nothing, yet later to find major cracks in the foundation?

Acceptance

The grief was heavy and difficult to sift through, but I eventually accepted that I had only one option: embrace my new reality and move forward.

I began asking myself some difficult questions: Was I living out any particular purpose, or was I coasting? Was I living confidently and boldly, or was I living out of fear, coloring only inside the lines? Was I taking control over my own story, or was I taking a backseat to my story?

Maybe I would have still attempted to hike the Camino, even if I had not been diagnosed with breast cancer. But I'm guessing I wouldn't have. My diagnosis was the catalyst. Though it has obviously come with its own set of challenges, I am, in some ways, thankful for the diagnosis because it sent me on the journey.

Many will focus on the heaviness and tragic nature of cancer, and I am not going to downplay its grim realities. But cancer also has a way of awakening you to the depth, beauty, and potential of life on a level you have not seen before.

That's not to say I was wasting my life before. I had a great husband and three wonderful kids, traveled a lot, and worked a good job. Life was good! All I'm saying is that had it not been for my cancer diagnosis, I would not have felt the urgency to do what I knew I needed to do: follow the voice that was calling to me so that I could figure out exactly how I wanted the rest of my life to be—how I wanted to live it, say it, and be it. So that I could, like Saint James, live with a boldness and conviction in whatever time I have left in life.

I had a lot to think about and some decisions to make about how I wanted my new beginning to be. I hoped the Camino could help me get some clarity on these things. I found myself beginning again— beginning a new phase of life, post-diagnosis—and stepping into the unknown of the journey, having no idea how or when it would end.

I found myself ready to move forward, yet a little leery for the journey ahead, not at all sure how it was going to go, but determined to give it my best shot.

- 2 -
The First Third

*"The universe buries strange jewels deep within us all and then
stands back to see if we can find them."*
-Elizabeth Gilbert, *Big Magic*

There's only so much training you can do to prepare for something like the Camino when you live in the suburbs of Chicago.

Leading up to my departure to Spain, I religiously did cardio and weight training and also hiked twenty-four miles in a single day with two of my walking buddies, Ann and Adele, around Lake Geneva, Wisconsin, which gave me a big boost of confidence. After that, I was sure I was ready.

All this to say, I figured that if I could get through the first leg of the Camino, there was a good chance I'd be able to make it all the way to Santiago, unless there was some unfortunate twist of the ankle or another unforeseen circumstance.

The Camino Frances throws you into the fire right off the bat if you begin just over the border into France in Saint-Jean-Pied-de-Port, as I did. Camino enthusiasts agree that the first day is the most physically demanding day of the entire journey, which entails a fifteen-mile hike and a four thousand-foot ascent into the Pyrenees Mountains, through the beautiful little village of Orissan, and then a steep descent into the town of Roncesvalles. It kicks off the "physical" leg of the Camino: the first third of the journey. The second third is the mental leg. The final third is the spiritual leg. Each section takes eleven to fourteen days, on average. Similarly, Kerry Egan, in her book *Fumbling - A Pilgrimage Tale of Love, Grief, and Spiritual Renewal on the Camino de Santiago*, likens the three parts of the Camino to birth and life, death, and resurrection. Indeed those parallels can be made and provide potential for deep metaphor as one walks the journey from France through Spain, 500 miles westward to Santiago.

"You don't walk the Camino; the Camino walks you. You talk to who you are supposed to talk to, you room with who you are supposed to room with, and you feel the pain you are supposed to feel."

Though some people begin in Pamplona instead of Saint-Jean-Pied-de-Port so they can skip the difficult hike up the Pyrenees, I was determined to walk the whole way, in hopes of pushing myself to the limits in this new beginning of my life. I am so glad I did. I will admit that it was hard, though. As I climbed up into the Pyrenees, which was as beautiful as it was painful, people were dragging, walking at a snail's pace uphill, and suffering from the heat of the day.

Even with the difficulty, the beauty of the Pyrenees lightens the load. The mountain views...the beautiful blue sky...the cows...the horses...and the sheep grazing in the green fields—none of it should be overlooked. Though my legs and feet ached with stiffness and overall fatigue, it was worth it to have the privilege of being one—united—with that unspoiled part of the world, if only for a little while.

On the climb to the peak of the Pyrenees, I met Dave, from Ireland, who told me something that stuck with me: "You don't walk the Camino; the Camino walks you. You talk to who you are supposed to talk to, you room with who you are supposed to room with, and you feel the pain you are supposed to feel."

This was Dave's second time walking the Camino, so I took what he said to be wise words. I decided then that I would make a special effort to just let it all unfold as it would. I would not lament pain or discomfort, I would enjoy every moment possible, and I would simply let what was going to happen, happen.

Breast Density

Like the Camino, my journey into the world of breast cancer screening discovery began with my own unfortunate pain. Pain can either hold us back or propel us forward. And, like Dave had suggested to me that first day in the Pyrenees, perhaps pain is something that each of us is "supposed to feel" to wake up to the truth, to take control over our own journey, and possibly use to help others.

When I returned from the Mayo Clinic and began to contemplate how shocked I was at all I had learned, I began obsessively researching breast cancer screening. What I ultimately found was that, just as walking the Camino begins with the physical leg, the effectiveness of breast cancer screening has to do with the physical makeup of the breast. I quickly discovered that there is much research that concludes that mammography will find *fewer than half* of all cancers in approximately half of all women.

It all came down to this: breast density. As the Mayo Clinic has described, "Breast tissue is composed of milk glands, milk ducts, supportive tissue (dense breast tissue), and fatty tissue (non-dense breast tissue). When viewed on a mammogram, women with dense breasts have more dense tissue than fatty tissue."[2]

"Women with extremely dense breasts are four to six times more likely to get breast cancer compared to women with fatty breasts. And 71 percent of all breast cancers are in women with dense breasts."

On a mammogram, non-dense breast tissue appears grey to black,[3] which is why mammograms do a very good job of finding breast cancers in non-dense breasts. Because breast cancer appears white on a mammogram, 98 percent of cancers are found in women with non-dense breast tissue because white stands out very well against the darker background tissue. That's great!

---

2. "Breast Density—The Four Levels," Mayo Clinic, Mayo Foundation for Medical Education and Research, www.mayoclinic.org/breast-density-mdash-the-four-levels/img-20008862.
3. "Dense Breast Tissue May Increase the Risk of Breast Cancer." Mayo Clinic, Mayo Foundation for Medical Education and Research, March 23, 2018, www.mayoclinic.org/tests-procedures/mammogram/in-depth/dense-breast-tissue/art-20123968.

But dense breast tissue, on the other hand, appears white on a mammogram—and so does cancer. That makes it difficult for radiologists to see what might be behind or intertwined with the dense tissue. This is why fewer than half of all cancers in dense breasts are found via mammography. That's not great!

Through my investigation, I learned that some women are now beginning to understand breast density, but many are still completely unaware. And even if they are aware, they have not yet learned that having dense breasts puts them at a higher risk for getting breast cancer. I was shocked to learn that having dense breasts is a significant risk factor for developing breast cancer. No one had ever told me that before.

There was a time when women thought they were unusual or it was their fault for having dense breasts. But the truth is that some of us have dense breasts, and others of us do not; any amount of breast density is normal. Further complicating breast density is that it can change with age and other factors. Two-thirds of pre-menopausal women have dense breasts, while one-fourth of post-menopausal women also have dense breasts. Spanning all ages, that's close to half of all women.[4]

Now, for some stats about breast density and cancer. This might be where the pain that you are supposed to feel sinks in. I share this with you not to create fear, but rather to inspire action. Women with extremely dense breasts are *four* to *six* times more likely to get breast cancer compared to women with fatty breasts. And 71 percent of all breast cancers are in women with dense breasts. So, not only does mammography often fail at finding cancers in women with dense breasts, as was the case with me, but it fails the women who need screening the most—those more likely to develop breast cancer.

The knowledge that breast density masks cancer in mammograms is not new information. Breast density has been understood for many years. Though many people are working diligently to make a difference in the lives of those who have dense breasts, progress to help women with dense breasts find cancer earlier when it is curable, however, has been way too slow in coming. Painfully slow, in fact.

Most women, as I did, think that an "all clear" mammogram means they don't have breast cancer, which simply might not be true, espe-

---

4. "Early Matters," Are You Dense?, www.areyoudense.org/.

cially if you have dense breasts. What it does mean is that no cancer was "seen," or "found," not necessarily that there is no cancer present.

Though I was diagnosed at age fifty-five, my doctors suspect that the cancer has been there for a long time, perhaps a decade or longer, because I have a slow-growing grade of a slow-growing kind of cancer. The cancerous area in my breast had grown to about three by five centimeters, which is about the size of an egg, completely masked by the dense tissue where it was hiding.

"A Failure of Our Technology"

As I learned all this in the wake of my diagnosis, I became understandably frustrated. If mammograms are so poor at seeing cancer in so many women, then why don't we have another way of looking? I also got an ultrasound, and that didn't see it, either! And if cancer being masked by dense breast tissue isn't new information, then why didn't I know about it?

Upon final discussion of the diagnosis with my doctor at the Mayo Clinic, he closed by saying, "This is not a failure of anyone, but this is a failure of our technology."

Although this may not be such a profound statement to others, it certainly was downright alarming to me.

The more I researched breast density, the more I came to understand that he was right. His statement summed it up perfectly. After all, when I transferred my mammogram images to the Mayo Clinic for their review, they concluded, "In the pictures you provided, we don't see the cancer, either."

Radiologists couldn't see past the white veil of dense breast tissue where the cancer was hidden. That was not because any of them were bad at their job; rather, it was because the technology that was being used to capture the images simply didn't reveal what was being obstructed by dense breast tissue. You can't expect anyone to actually see something that isn't there on the imaging, and this is how it can be with cancer in mammogram images and dense breast tissue.

There is plenty to be mad about in all this, that's for sure, but I just didn't want to take that fork in the road. As sad as I was, I wasn't terribly angry. I did, however, sense that I had encountered a hole in the breast cancer screening system, one that many women, including me, might suffer dire consequences for. I wanted to learn more about how and why women all over were suffering the consequences of such a "failure of our technology," and why, then, weren't we coming up with a better way to detect breast cancer?

There was so much more to learn.

A New Technology

At this point, I thought, "If we don't have a good enough way to find breast cancer at early stages in women who have dense breast tissue, then we need to *create* the technology to do so." It was neither an incredibly brilliant nor novel thought, but logical nonetheless. I knew I couldn't be the first "rocket scientist" to come up with this conclusion, so what in the world was going on?

One morning while I was browsing through the Mayo Clinic app on my phone, I saw an article about something called Molecular Breast Imaging—MBI for short. It was an eye-opening article, backed by science and research, offering a ray of hope for women like me with dense breasts. MBI was created specifically to combat the limitations of mammography due to breast density and had been approved by the FDA for screening a few years before. The article claimed that MBI found *363 percent* more cancers when added to standard mammography in women with dense breasts.[5]

I found this to be astounding, exciting, and somewhat maddening all at the same time. How in the world had I never heard of this? And if MBI finds that many more cancers than mammography in dense breasts, then that said a lot about how many are currently being left undetected. I could not help but wonder if things might have turned out differently for me if I had been given access to this technology years earlier. Likely so, but there is no way to know for sure.

To some, this might be discouraging to seemingly miss out on a new wave of technology. In the end, though, I was more encouraged than I was disheartened. There was nothing I could do to change my situation. Each of us must ultimately own our own story, no matter how it unfolds.

What I did do, however, was immediately text all my friends to tell

---

5. "Molecular Breast Imaging FAQ." Molecular Breast Imaging FAQ-Mayo Clinic Health System, www.mayoclinichealthsystem.org/hometown-health/speaking-of-health/molecular-breast-imaging-faq.

them about this new way of finding breast cancer that they should look into if they had dense breasts. I couldn't change my story, but I could do my best to make sure that my story didn't become their story.

A Chance Encounter

Not long after reading the article, I returned to Mayo to attend their "Healthy Living Program" to determine the best diet, exercise, and overall wellness for my particular condition.

At the end of the program, the doctors at Mayo make sure that you walk away with tailored plans for cardio workouts, strength training, and diet guidelines, all geared to you specifically. A doctor is also assigned to each person to oversee the process. The doctor who was assigned to me that day was a woman named Deborah J. Rhodes, MD.[6]

Dr. Rhodes met with me briefly in the morning and explained the details of the day. Then we reconvened again in the afternoon to finalize a strategy together. It was then that she said to me, "I read through your files and looked at all the records you've provided. You are the woman I have dedicated my career to for the past ten years." I was taken aback, touched, and of course intensely curious.

She went on to explain that she was a lead inventor of Molecular Breast Imaging. I couldn't believe she was one of the architects behind the technology I had *just* read about days before on the Mayo Clinic app! What were the chances?

What happened with me—having cancer hidden by dense breast tissue—was exactly what she and others were trying to prevent and why they were so persistent in trying to perfect this technology and get it out into the world. When she said that to me, I suddenly realized I was not the only one who had this story, but that I represent the many women out there like me whose cancers are found later than they should be—some too late to be saved.

Dr. Rhodes also told me about a new study she had begun called Density MATTERS. It was to be conducted over two to three years on three thousand women at seven different sites. These widespread massive studies are the very thing the medical community wants to see

---

6. "Faculty: Deborah J. Rhodes, MD," Mayo Clinic, https://www.mayo.edu/research/faculty/rhodes-deborah-j-m-d/bio-00027482.

to prove that they should accept any new idea or technology, like MBI. The Density MATTERS study compares the performance of Molecular Breast Imaging (MBI) to that of 3D mammography, also called DBT (Digital Breast Tomography), or tomosynthesis. The study seeks to prove that MBI finds more cancers than 3D mammography, that it costs less per cancer found, and that it does so with equal radiation. Additionally, MBI costs about the same as 3D mammography, while an MRI (Magnetic Resonance Imaging, which also finds many cancers) costs four to five times that of a 3D mammogram or an MBI. Preliminary results of the Density MATTERS study were already extremely promising, but unfortunately, the study was not completely funded.

There was still a lot of work to be done, but I was thrilled nonetheless. So there actually *was* something else that not only was much better at detecting cancer in dense breasts, but was as cost effective as 3D mammography as well: MBI. That felt like major progress to me at the time, but clearly there was work to be done for all women to have access to the benefits this new technology provides.

An Opportunity

I had been mulling the idea around in my head about fundraising for a breast-cancer-related cause as I walked the Camino. Logic might tell you that I would raise funds for the study I am a subject in at the Mayo Clinic called PROMISE.[7]

PROMISE uses participants' biopsies to obtain detailed information regarding the genetic makeup of the tumor, with the goal of developing personalized treatment approaches to improve patient outcomes. That is important work, to be sure, and I am happy to contribute to it. But something drew me to being a part, if only in a very small way, of helping our sisters, friends, daughters, mothers, and coworkers benefit from a better way of finding breast cancer, one that could potentially save lives. I could not stop thinking about Dr. Rhodes's Density MATTERS study. Helping to fund this study, I thought, might be the best and most impactful way for me to make a difference.

I felt like I should follow my gut.

---

7. "Breast Cancer: PROMISE Study," Mayo Clinic, https://www.mayo.edu/research/centers-programs/center-individualized-medicine/patient-care/clinical-studies/promise.

I felt like I should listen to my heart.

This was something that could fill the exact hole I saw in the system, and it was "right there," so close to being widely accessible and benefiting so many women who will come after me. So close, but not close enough.

That day, I could tell that Dr. Rhodes was deeply passionate about her work. But any advances in the medical field can take a long time to become widely accepted, and I couldn't imagine the patience that was required of her. She remarked that day, "I will die trying to get this technology out into the world."

"No, I think you will die having done it," I said, believing her passion, intelligence, and courage would eventually lead to fruition.

I also thought, "And maybe I can help."

That was the moment that I decided to fundraise for the Density MATTERS study.

Because of the scientific, political, and financial ramifications, it takes forever for new findings in the medical community to become widely accepted. It also takes a lot of time and money to move the needle even slightly. That was the only discouraging thing I felt that day in hearing about all this: realizing just how long research and the widespread adoption of findings actually takes.

To add to the complexity, it's important to note that insurance carriers are only required to cover 2D mammography under the Affordable Care Act, so there may be an additional out-of-pocket cost for MBI, 3D mammography, or MRI. Medicare and insurance carriers are slowly, yet increasingly, covering supplemental screenings such as these. MBI screening costs approximately the same as a 3D mammogram while MRI, on average, costs about five times more than a 3D mammogram or MBI. It is all very confusing. No wonder there is a status quo. No wonder women with dense breasts wind up settling for mammograms even if they only find less than half of cancers present. No wonder women aren't aware of other options. Something needs to change.

But in all this, I saw an opportunity: just as Dr. Rhodes was trying to create inertia in the scientific and medical community, what if I could also create inertia in the public among women who were just like me? We are nowhere near having women everywhere with access to a technology that actually sees most of their breast cancers, no matter what their breast density, for a price equal to 3D mammography.

But creating awareness can change that.

In a strange way, although I was dealing with a devastating diagnosis, I felt a new invigoration with a fire in my heart and a fullness in my lungs. Taking one's own misfortunes and using them to help others certainly can lift the spirit, and for me at that time, it felt right to do just that. Just as Dr. Rhodes had dedicated her career to women like me, I felt within me a longing to do the same.

Maybe in some instances, mammography was like shining light through concrete, but it felt like my two doctors at Mayo were shining a light down a dark path for me to follow, pointing me in the direction I needed to go. I had so much more to learn and to say, and I needed time away to organize my priorities, thoughts, and shed some baggage that would be too heavy to carry into this next phase of my life. The Camino was there to give me the time and space to do that. So I walked...and walked...uphill and downhill...and then walked some more. A *lot* more.

- 3 -
Into the Unknown

"Have no fear of moving into the unknown. Simply step out fearlessly knowing that I am with you, therefore no harm can befall you; all is very, very well. Do this in complete faith and confidence."
-Pope John Paul II

I think one of the reasons the Camino found me was because of the mystery that the Camino is and the mystery that my life's unfolding had become. The farther I walked that first leg, the more I felt as if I were stepping further into the unknown. How long would the hike last? What would it be like? Did I have what it takes physically, mentally, and emotionally to hike the whole Camino?

Then there were the deeper "cancer" questions that came to my mind as I walked: "Why me? Why did this happen?"

But then I found myself reframing the questions: "Why not me?" Maybe I was someone who could help others. Maybe I was someone who could help save lives.

And if I am someone who can help make a difference, someone who can help women with dense breast tissue learn about other kinds of screening so they can get the reliable screening they deserved, then maybe it was time to step up to the plate.

The truth is that none of us has control over our lives like we think we do. Nonetheless, there's something about Stage 4 cancer that makes you realize your finitude. And the Camino reminds you what life really is at its core: a journey and a mystery. In those first few days during the physically straining leg of the journey, I noticed that a number of people, especially from the United States, wanted to know exactly how far each hike was, how high they were climbing, and where they were staying every night.

They wanted the details so that they could plan out their days and set their expectations, as if having that kind of knowing, that kind of control, was better than not having it. They would become anxious whenever they had to succumb to simply moving forward without thinking they knew what lay ahead. To them, it felt aimless and uncalculated, but the truth is that the path was right in front of them all along, beckoning them to simply take one step after another. The Camino isn't about the destination. If you make it about the destination, you'll miss out on the very best part of the Camino.

Anticipatory Grief

In my own life, I can usually tell whenever I am obsessing over something that I can't control because there is a certain weight that accompanies me. I call it "anticipatory grief"—grieving over something that I think I might lose later but have not lost yet. This is a common emotion that we all have, at least to some degree.

I have especially felt this as a mother when my children have faced a problem, and I have felt helpless or lost in trying to solve the situation for them. I lay in bed wide-eyed many nights, playing out each worst-case scenario, one followed by another, pushed along by fear, which only multiplies my worry and angst. Before I know it, I'm grieving ten different things that have not even happened yet.

On the Camino, at times you can't tell where the path is headed. Sometimes there is a fork in the road in the distance, and you aren't sure which is the right direction—there are no visible signs telling you which way to go. Sometimes the path ahead disappears into the hills or spins you around amid the challenging terrain, blurring your sense of direction. Sometimes the path dissolves into a town or a city.

I learned while walking all those miles of twists and turns that worrying about the fork in the road ahead before I got there was of no use; that the direction to take would become evident in due time. There was no point in worrying about something in the distance when everything would become apparent once I got there. I realized that no matter where I was on the Camino, I was surrounded by the splendor of both culture and nature, and I had a choice: to savor and enjoy each moment or to worry about what was to come.

I translated this quite quickly to my own lack of knowing about the future progression of my cancer. I concluded that, like on the Camino, anticipatory grief was not going to be my friend. I had too much life left to live. Why spend my time worrying about tomorrow and allow that to rob me of a full life today?

After all, you never know what is going to happen. A new medicine could come out tomorrow, or a cure could be found next year. Why waste my energy worrying about things I cannot control? Although I did not have words for it until I wrote this book, I think I found myself on the Camino not only looking to have a fuller, bolder, and more exciting future, but also to confront the unknown, fully live that out, and reframe my mental approach to life.

Hold It Loosely

Before I left for the Camino, Rev. Laurie Michaels, a deacon at St. Michael's Episcopal Church in Barrington, Illinois, gave me some very good words of wisdom: "Hold it loosely," she said to me one day after church service, days away from my departure to Spain.

It became something of a mantra for me as I both wrestled with my diagnosis and as I hiked the Camino. Letting go of some things—or holding them loosely—so that I might be able to embrace other things, became a recurring thought for me as I walked the endless miles of the Camino. And I must say, that mind-set shift has served me well, both during the Camino journey and afterward.

The more you cling to anything, the worse the situation can get. Hold onto any material object, expectation, narrative, or idea too closely, and it will likely eventually create some sort of problem. On the Camino, you can worry about a mountainous section twenty days down the road, perhaps a specific part that you are concerned about, but is that beneficial now? Your legs will feel different twenty days down the road. Your stamina will be different twenty days down the road. Worrying about the unknown takes up space in your brain, and it is debilitating.

I decided to hold most everything more loosely so I could fully embrace the joy, contentment, and opportunity in the moments as I moved on through the journey.

Letting Go of a Narrative

Like those on the Camino who were obsessed with schedules and plans because it gave them needed certainty, the equivalent behavior, as I see it in the breast cancer screening world, is the clinging to—for dear life sometimes—the narrative, or even the myth, of the mammogram.

It has been known for years that dense breast tissue masks cancer in mammograms. Yet we have held onto the narrative that mammograms are a "gold standard," so we have clung to it...so very tightly. Likely to the peril of many women.

Mammograms have saved many lives, and I hope one has saved your life or that of someone you love dearly. But when can we hold on a bit more loosely, let go, and open up to the idea that mammograms do not do that for everyone, and never have? When can we embrace that instead of fight it?

What's holding the medical community back? Admitting the old story wasn't as good as we once thought it was? An unclear way forward? High profits generated from fully depreciated equipment? Fear? Or maybe being overwhelmed by the sheer volume of all of the constant changes in medicine? Limited budgets? Or is it simply that change is hard, and we usually don't do it until we have to, even if we know better?

What if we could hold mammography just a bit more loosely? To open up some space for what could come, something that could get us back to our core purpose of finding as many breast cancers as early as possible, so that more women with breast cancer could become survivors? What if we could hold today just a little more loosely, just enough to let that idea in? To let go of the present and make our way just a bit farther down the road toward better early detection, toward saving more of the lives of our daughters, mothers, sisters, and friends?

Since its invention in the 1960s, mammography has moved us forward as a society in the desire to reduce breast cancer mortality. Many lives have been saved, and the mortality rate from breast cancer per year in the United States has gone from around 72,000 back then, to around 41,000 per year now. But unfortunately, those numbers have plateaued, and it's time to make the next leap.

If our journey is to find every breast cancer early to decrease the mortality, we have to let go of where we are so we can move forward. That involves holding things a bit more loosely and letting go of one thing so we can embrace something else. In this case, that means admitting that mammography alone is not the best we can do for the many women with dense breasts. That is easier said than done, of course, because this is a very messy space full of varying and biased opinions, protection of profits and relationships, conflicting medical boards, cost versus profits, and fear of lawsuits.

What could turn the tide? What could push us over the edge from clinging so tightly to holding this narrative just a little more loosely?

Creating a New Narrative

I am not a doctor. I am not a researcher. But what I can do is help women become more aware of advanced screening and help them demand the breast cancer screening they so very much deserve to have.

Imagine if every woman called up her local hospital and asked, "Do you offer functional breast screening, such as MBI or MRI? If you don't, I'm going somewhere else that will."

That will change things.

But I think that we, as women and patients, are tied to that mammogram story as well, though in a different way, and understandably so. We, too, have to let go of our own narrative that says, "I got my mammogram, so I am all good. Whew!" We so want that to be true because that's what we've been told for years, and it's so much easier just to believe it. When our doctors call us and say, "All good, see you next year," what we really hear is, "I don't have breast cancer." I certainly was happy to think that! Until I couldn't anymore...

Honestly, though, it might be very upsetting to some women and doctors to accept that we now need to see things differently because that would mean realizing that what we have been told all along may not actually be true all of the time. But inspiring a new narrative is what it is going to take to shift the forces of money, power, and control, and all those who cling so tightly. Confronting the truth head-on is what it's going to take. This means not believing an advertisement that promises peace of mind for those with dense breasts with 3D mammography and ultrasound—because it doesn't. It means not taking our doctor's word for it when he or she tells us all we need is 3D mammography when we have dense breasts because it's the new "gold standard" in mammography—because we shouldn't. This means advocating for ourselves, because we must. This means learning about and deciding what we want, and having the courage to get it, regardless of the resistance we might encounter.

> "On the Camino, you realize very quickly what is most important to you on your journey. If you get too hung up on all the details, you'll miss out on exploring why you're on the Camino to begin with. For healing. For transformation. For growth. For progress."

I do, however, empathize with the medical industry and those who are so attached to the mammogram narrative. People who are paid to make business decisions have invested millions of dollars into this narrative because they, too, were told that it was the gold standard of breast cancer screening. Hospitals have spent millions of dollars on mammography equipment and have gone all in with this narrative to help their patients. Manufacturers, too, have spent millions on making the equipment, and it's likely they were doing it to help people. As a society, we've invested in the narrative when the reality is that mammograms have been oversold.

So the question is this: Are we content with 41,000 women dying from breast cancer every year?

No one is going to say yes to that, but do we actually have the will to change it? Embracing (and demanding) new technology in addition to mammograms is a good place to start.

The Only Direction on the Journey Is Forward

It is time for us, as a culture that supposedly elevates equality and takes pride in innovation, to hold today loosely so we can fully embrace a better tomorrow.

On the Camino, you realize very quickly what is most important to you on your journey. If you get too hung up on all the details, you'll miss out on exploring why you're on the Camino to begin with. For healing. For transformation. For growth. For progress.

In marrying ourselves too tightly to the mammogram story, and clinging to all that holds us there, we have likely lost sight of the fact that we are on a journey to save as many women from dying from breast cancer as we possibly can. The way we do that has to change as we progress down the road toward saving more and more lives. We have to let go of what we clung to yesterday on the journey so we can fully embrace today and tomorrow, lest we collectively forget why we are on this path to begin with. For healing. For saving lives. For patients. For moving humanity forward. And so more women with breast cancer become survivors.

- 4 -
Solo

"Freeing yourself was one thing, claiming ownership of that freed self was another."
-Toni Morrison, *Beloved*

I entered the Camino dedicated to venturing into the unknown, determined to learn to like it, and focused on making it my Camino—my own journey and no one else's. I fully intended to make time for myself so I could solidify where I wanted to take my life and how I could best help other women like me, even if it wasn't crystal clear what that would look like.

In the busyness of our culture and the havoc of everything that had transpired in my own life, I knew some good time alone, the therapeutic aspect of distance walking, beautiful scenery, and lots of fresh air was just what I needed. I had allowed my heart to carry me onto the Camino but knew I needed to uncover its potential—the treasures within. Uncovering the desires in my heart and unleashing them, I knew, would entail some difficult inner work.

Up to that point, I had never been particularly good at making enough space for solitude. The issue wasn't that I was scared to be alone; I actually loved it. But when I was not on my own, I tended to slip into whatever role I sensed the group needed me to play—even if I didn't want to play that role—and then I struggled to wrangle out of it, knowing the resistance or pushback I would face. I wanted to leave that pattern behind, and walking the Camino by myself was a firm first step.

The Role We're Expected to Play

I think many of us, particularly women, often fail to make time for ourselves because we are so often expected to do too much for others—to be all things to all people whenever they need it.

"No" is a word we don't use often enough, and there is an undercurrent in our society that reinforces that. The result is that it is "everybody else" first, and it's possible to lose ourselves along the way. On one hand, this is why we're so good at multitasking. But on the other, it's why we often feel like we have to go along with the "way things are" and wind up feeling taken advantage of.

> *"I had allowed my heart to carry me onto the Camino but knew I needed to uncover its potential—the treasures within. Uncovering the desires in my heart and unleashing them, I knew, would entail some difficult inner work."*

My generation was really the first to break into the workforce and work full-time jobs in significant numbers, but that didn't change things as much as you'd think. We were still expected to do what our mothers and grandmothers had done before: take care of the kids, keep the house in order, cook, and clean—all of it. Gender roles were still as strong as ever, and eventually, it got the best of me, which then led to me having to walk away from my job. This saddened me because I enjoyed "working" my product development job, and I was really good at it.

For much of my life, I've felt trapped by societal expectations and by traditional gender roles, but I had not been able to break out of it in a way that suited me. Since my diagnosis, however, I had settled on this conclusion: I don't want to feel this trap anymore, so I am going to figure out how not to feel it. After a Stage 4 cancer diagnosis, if you aren't going to change something that's been bugging you for years, you probably aren't ever going to. Now, if ever, would be the time.

My decision to hike the Camino alone arose, in part, out of this determined and empowered mind-set. Most people respected it, although only some understood it. Women who had pretty much lived a life like mine were the most likely to get it, saying, "Oh yeah, I get that totally! You go, girlfriend!" Others, usually men, wondered why my husband "let me go." But with that said, many men were incredibly supportive, and a few women, not so much. My very unofficial yet probably accurate tally while on the Camino was that more men than women walk it alone, and those women walking it alone were at least a couple decades younger than me. This is probably a direct result of the tired idea that women should not travel alone, or do anything alone, because if they do, there must be something wrong with them. Or that they should not travel alone because the world is dangerous, which is not completely untrue, and that we should be scared and probably sit back, even if we really want to go.

But for me, Stage 4 cancer was pretty scary, and those of us living with it need some bravery, so it was time to muster some courage and hike the Camino, for starters. Compared to cancer, walking a long way in a relatively safe country with many other pilgrims walking toward Saint James's relics seemed like a pretty safe thing to do. No real comparison there.

It was time to buck the "system," stop worrying about what everyone else needed or thought, and just do it. And so I went. By myself. Alone. And loved it.

The Breakaway

For all pilgrims, the walking journey on the Camino can provide many metaphors for life, should the pilgrim choose to see them as such. My first Camino lesson, if you will, came very early on.

On that first treacherous day of hiking up and down the Pyrenees, I met a few people along the way, and then a few more at the *albergue* that first night. *Albergues* are accommodations specifically for pilgrims and generally consist of rooms with a large number of single or bunk beds.

In situations like these, a lot of bonding can happen quickly. Seven of us decided we'd head out the next morning and walk together.

This was a fun group, and I was happy to meet some new friends. The group consisted of two single guys and a couple from Ireland, a couple from California, and me. It was a curious yet somehow compatible group of people. We shared a lot of stories and had some good laughs. Two of them were on their second Camino pilgrimage and provided us first-timers with a lot of Camino tips, pointers, and wisdom. One of them even gave me his guidebook, which turned out to be the best thing ever because it was so much better than the guidebook I had.

The next morning we headed out early, before dawn. The two single Irish men were absolutely certain we needed to do this to beat the crowd and ensure that we got a bed the next night; we'd had trouble with that the night before.

We walked hard all day long that day in the heat, up and down, on rocky terrain, not really stopping for lunch or many breaks, so we could "get ahead" of the crowd. I was tired, always the last one pulling up the rear. There was no time to stop to savor the beauty of our surroundings, rest our feet, or rejuvenate. I felt rushed and out of sorts. I went along with it for a while because I was used to doing that in my life—but not for long.

As we walked into Pamplona on the third day around noon, the group was hell-bent on blowing right through the city in a big hurry. That's when I knew I had to say "no," an uncomfortable thing for me, and let them go, no matter how much I disliked the idea of probably never seeing them again. Simply put, I had come to realize that I was walking *their* Camino, not mine, and I knew I needed to take action. It was a little sad, but mostly liberating, knowing that I was going to stay true to totally doing it my way, on my own time.

People flow in and out of our lives. Some stay a long time, and some are with us for only a moment. I was grateful that I had gotten to know these lovely people whom I consciously decided to let walk farther and farther ahead of me until they were out of sight. I would never catch up to them or see them again. I knew I'd miss their great Irish humor and the endearing brogue. And I knew I was better for having met them; they helped me realize that to forage one's own path might require letting go of some other things, or even people, to do it, and that is likely what is meant to be.

I decided to stop walking and stay in Pamplona, and it was definitely a step in the right direction.

Pamplona—Party of One

My mother once told me, "Learn to be your own best friend, and you'll never be lonely." So very true.

For the next two days, I stayed in Pamplona to rest and regroup. Most *albergues* consist of just a large room filled with bunk beds. But in

Pamplona, there was a little "room," basically the size of a twin bed with a shelf, a phone-charging outlet, and a privacy shade. I loved having my own little tiny room, which was really more like the size of a one-person tent. After three full days on the Camino, it felt downright luxurious. I got some writing done, talked to people at the *albergue* and on the streets, went to a Pilgrim's Mass at the cathedral, took a tour of the oldest bell tower in Spain, visited the "Running of the Bulls" plaza, and did my very own personal pub crawl. The Camino at its best is a perfect cocktail of solitude and community, and that's what I enjoyed so much those two days.

"Our relationships with others hinge on our relationship with ourselves. We can't take care of others if we don't take care of ourselves first."

I walked out of that city more determined to, for the rest of my journey, be able to answer the question, "Whose Camino are you walking: yours, or someone else's?" Oh yes, it was definitely going to be mine.

Our relationships with others hinge on our relationship with ourselves. We can't take care of others if we don't take care of ourselves first. That's why a lot of caretakers often lose themselves and why people who work at nonprofits or churches get burnt out so quickly.

I also think it's easier for women to slip into that role. Whether it's nature or nurture, I'm not sure, but a lot of us just seem to put our own well-being on the back burner. I know a lot of women who feel guilty whenever they care for themselves and make sure they get what they need. It might feel selfish, but it's not. It is an absolute necessity.

So I ask you: Whose Camino are you walking?

You Own It

Just as I needed to take control of my Camino journey, so it goes with breast cancer screening for every woman as well. Not that this is easy, because it certainly isn't.

When it comes to our healthcare, we all tend to do whatever our physicians tell us, no questions asked. Generally speaking, we are afraid to ask questions. We are afraid to put a foot down and say what we want. We can be afraid to take ownership of our own medical journeys.

Maybe it's because of the complexity of the healthcare system. Maybe it's because of how small we feel when doctors quickly pop into our screening rooms, deliver a trite analysis, and then quickly move on. Maybe it's because of the underlying fear each of us has when we go to the doctor, that we might be told that something is wrong. It's easier not to ask questions. It's easier not to say what we want.

It's easier to just get a mammogram, trust the result, and happily forget it until the next year. If we step up and probe further, asking for supplemental tests and more in-depth screening, then there's the chance they might find something. Perhaps more than any other field, the medical arena might be the most intimidating, and one that most of us understand the least.

And particularly in the case of mammography and breast cancer in general, there is so much conflicting, biased, confusing, and some-times downright wrong information out there that it is hard to know precisely what to ask for, even if we're inclined to. Unfortunately, even the experts can't agree.

Right now, there is no agreement among all medical boards about exactly what is the right breast cancer screening for women with dense breasts. The American College of Radiology disagrees with the United States Preventive Services Task Force, and neither of them aligns completely with the American Society of Breast Surgeons. It goes on and on from there. It is confusing for patients and doctors at best and detrimental to our health at worst. I have concluded at this point that "they" aren't going to decide among themselves on our behalf, so we've got to do it ourselves.

When it comes to our own breast cancer screening, we've got to break away from the pack and own it ourselves. If we don't, nobody else will.

Be Your Own Breast Friend

It's awfully hard to be your best self—doing what you do best—if you have breast cancer. But the earlier it's found, the better off you obviously are in the long term. Stage 0 breast cancer treatment can be faster and easier than Stages 2 and 3, and it's certainly a far cry from Stage 4 treatment. Early detection is also critical to overall survival.[8]

---

8. "What Does Prognosis Mean?" Breastcancer.org, January 26, 2017. https://www.breastcancer.org/symptoms/diagnosis/prognosis.

So for your own health and well-being, you've got to be your own breast friend and do all you can to find breast cancer early, should you happen to be among the one in eight women (on average) who will get breast cancer in her lifetime. This starts with you. It's *for* you. It's *about* you. So how are you going to own your own breast-cancer-screening story?

As I've discussed, clearly knowing your breast density is a place to start. And to know that, you must start with a mammogram, 3D (or DBT) if available, and then go from there.

As you likely know by now, it might not be easy to understand what you need and then ultimately get it. Some doctors could be as much as ten years behind on the latest treatments and technologies. They are often busy, overworked, and unable to keep up with the rapidly changing technologies and treatments. Their performance is sometimes measured by how many people they see in a day, and this can be just as frustrating for them as it is for you. You might need to switch doctors to be heard.

You also might have to push back on your insurance company. You might need to insist. You might need to call them many times. You might, in fact, have to use your outdoor voice inside. We've all got one of those, and the time to use it is certainly warranted in defending your own health. However, in general, insurance companies are paying more and more for supplemental screening for women with dense breasts because they are beginning to understand the "what if" scenario. That's good news!

It is frustrating to live in a country where it feels like those making decisions might not have our best interests in mind. However, one of the great things about this country is that demand always leads to change. We, as women, have the opportunity to increase the demand.

But it starts with each of us as we walk solo on our own path and take care of ourselves and own our own breast care. And our personal care and awareness overflows onto others, perhaps through telling a friend or a family member about what we've learned.

Take care of yourself first, and then help spread the word about breast density and supplemental screening. Why? So that one day there will be no need to educate others, no need to take on the insurance companies, and no need to insist on what is best for us…because then it will be the norm.

- 5 -
The Arena

*"When we spend our lives waiting until we're perfect or bulletproof
before we walk into the arena, we ultimately sacrifice relationships
and opportunities that may not be recoverable, we squander our
precious time, and we turn our backs on our gifts, those unique
contributions that only we can make. Perfect and bulletproof are
seductive, but they don't exist in the human experience."*
-Brené Brown, *Daring Greatly*

O n the Camino, you quickly see that most other people are carrying their own burdens and allowing the Camino to create the
space for their own internal work. This was certainly true for me, too.

The Camino removed me from the rest of the world's chaos and
clutter, creating the space for solitude and introspection, for genuine
relationships to form, and for personal growth to unfold. It helped me
see things more clearly so I could approach life with more clarity.

For example, trekking up the mountain that first day was empowering from a physical standpoint, and leaving the group and reclaiming
my journey several days in was empowering on an internal level. Not
only was the Camino creating the exterior space I needed to roam and
to discover God's beautiful creation, it was also providing the time for
me to confront some internal things, like the baggage I had been carrying and was eager to leave behind.

Perhaps the most evident representation of these burdens are the rocks that pilgrims carry around with them and eventually place at the foot of statues and crosses, all along the Camino. These rocks usually represent burdens or grief they are hoping to surrender and mentally release while on their journey.

Take Mary, for example, who looked for heart-shaped rocks on the trail, collected them, carried them, and then made shapes and statues out of those rocks scattered along the trail all the way to Santiago. Mary's divorce ended badly with a heart surgeon who ironically died of heart cancer. She was hoping that hiking the Camino would help her forgive, let go, and heal her own heart.

At the most famous of these crosses, Cruz de Ferro—an iron cross that sits at the highest point on the Camino Frances—I laid down a rock for each Purdue University Sigma Kappa sorority sister of mine who had died of breast cancer, including one who passed away while I was hiking. I added an additional rock for our best man's wife, who also passed away from breast cancer several years before. It was my way of paying tribute to those who had gone before me, and it was a promise to them that I would do what I could to help those coming after us. It was a somber yet moving experience.

While walking during the day or while talking at the restaurants, bars, or *albergues* in the evening, people would share their stories with one another. They talked about who they were honoring, why they were there, and what they were hoping to surrender by the end of the Camino. Not everyone had a reason. Some just wanted to hike the Camino simply as a life experience. But most had an intention of some sort, even if they didn't have words for it. Most on the Camino were in search of something within.

The Retreat That Paved the Way

A few years prior to my diagnosis, I attended a "Daring Way" retreat based on Brené Brown's best-selling book, *Daring Greatly*. During those miles and miles of walking on the Camino, I began to recall that retreat and the quote from Teddy Roosevelt, on which the book and the retreat are both based:

> It is not the critic who counts; not the man who points out how the strong man stumbles, or where the doer of deeds could have done them better. The credit belongs to the man

who is actually in the arena, whose face is marred by dust and sweat and blood; who strives valiantly; who errs, who comes short again and again, because there is no effort without error and shortcoming; but who does actually strive to do the deeds; who knows great enthusiasms, the great devotions; who spends himself in a worthy cause; who at the best knows in the end the triumph of high achievement, and who at the worst, if he fails, at least fails while daring greatly, so that his place shall never be with those cold and timid souls who neither know victory nor defeat.

Brown uses this quote as an incredible metaphor for stepping up and being bold in life…and all that comes along with this kind of boldness. She equates the reserved seats—or maybe the box seats—in the arena as those places where your best and most trusted supporters will sit, cheering you on, no matter what happens while you are out in the arena. Only a few of these seats are available, but it's important that at least some of those are filled. It is vital that we have those who are forever and always in our corner.

She also discusses those who are seated in the "cheap" seats, which unfortunately might be the largest crowd. These are those folks who are willing or even wanting to boo, laugh, throw popcorn at you, or otherwise diminish or discredit what you are trying to do, meanwhile playing it safe in the crowd, and doing nothing daring themselves. Anyone who has done anything daring at all knows there are plenty of people in the cheap seats.

All this and more is used as an analogy for us to think about what arena we'd like to enter, if we dare, and what's holding us back from entering it. These kinds of questions can only be answered—and this kind of introspection can only take place—if you make the space to consider what kind of heaviness you might be carrying around with you.

Breaking Down the Armor

Brené Brown also talks a lot about the armor we wear for protection against the fear of those in the cheap seats. That armor can come in the form of justification, excuses, or any other elaborate reason why we can't, shouldn't, or don't want to be in the arena.

People generally wear the proverbial armor because they are afraid—afraid to share what is in the deep recesses of their heart. They construct armor to shield the vulnerable parts of themselves from criticism, embarrassment, or opposition. But the thing about armor is that it's heavy. There's no letting others see the dreams, passions, love, and joy residing within whenever they are shielded by bulky armor. My armor was definitely heavy, and I was quite ready to shed it. It was weighing me down.

I guess you could say my armor was constructed of doubt. I had all kinds of doubts about sharing what was on my heart and mind about breast cancer screening. I was not a writer. I was not a speaker. I was not a doctor or a researcher. I was an older woman—a fifty-five-year-old mother and former product manager—from the Midwest. Would I be taken seriously? Would anyone listen? How could someone like me really make a difference?

Sometimes I heard the sexist voices of my past screaming at me from the cheap seats. The negative things that were said by others about women if they were, say, loud or opinionated or passionate. The criticisms that were made of women who weren't playing the role that society seemed to expect them to play.

Even as a kid, I subconsciously noted that there was a certain shame to speaking up, that men were more important when it came to leadership, and that there was a certain role I was expected to fulfill. As I grew older and worked in male-dominated spaces throughout the 1980s, the overt and covert sexist comments made in the workplace sometimes felt like a slow burn of the soul. It hurts each time, but you don't realize it until many years later that society has made you somewhat hollow. You don't realize the voices that you carry around or the weight of your doubt until you go inward to unleash something that is important to you.

Now I realize that all of this pales by comparison to having Stage 4 cancer and puts it right in perspective. If I can thrive with Stage 4 cancer, then I am confident that I can do almost anything. So thank you, cancer, for helping me shed my heavy armor…and for thrusting me out into the arena.

Almost all of us have armor of some sort. What is yours?

Stepping Up

On the Camino, I was wrestling with some of the world's injustices, specifically in the medical community. I was discouraged that many in that community knew dense breast tissue masks cancer on mammograms for years, yet very little was done about it. It was even debated as to whether women should be told about this or not.

The fact that this was even a debate is very telling about our culture. Had they shared what they had learned—what they knew to be true back then—instead of debating whether to tell women or not, then maybe I, along with tens of thousands of other women, wouldn't be in the situations we're in today.

I found myself coming face-to-face with the stark reality I've heard that a number of social justice advocates have to confront: how to live happily and try to make a difference in the world and not let those injustices bring you down on a daily basis. That's a hard balance. It's something of a burden. But it is important to keep stepping into the arena nonetheless.

There are many people who have and still are working very hard to make progress in breast cancer screening, but when I think of someone who particularly stepped out into the arena boldly and with incredible conviction, I think of Dr. Nancy Cappello. Dr. Cappello founded two organizations called Are You Dense, Inc. (www.areyoudense.org) and Are You Dense Advocacy, Inc. (www.areyoudenseadvocacy.org). In 2004, she was diagnosed with Stage 3c breast cancer six weeks after receiving a normal mammography report.

She helped pass the breast density disclosure law in Connecticut, the first in the nation, and dedicated the rest of her life to getting disclosure laws passed in thirty-six states that require radiologists to tell their patients if they have dense breasts. Because her cancer was Stage 3c, she had to undergo intense chemotherapy and harsh treatment. She ended up getting bone marrow cancer (MDS) as a result of the harsh realities of chemo. She

"Sometimes you don't even realize how heavy the armor is that you're wearing until you step out into the arena, and then you have to deconstruct the fear and worry that are holding you back so that you can be free to do what you are supposed to do."

died November 15, 2018.

She didn't live long enough to see Senator Dianne Feinstein place a requirement in the 2019 appropriations bill stating that the FDA must redo its guidelines regarding breast density. Those changes are supposed to be implemented in 2021. No matter your politics, this is a big win for women everywhere.

Despite all the frustration, pushback, and the other "stuff" hurled at her from the cheap seats, Dr. Cappello stepped into the arena and helped make something happen that will benefit all women. It's unfortunate that she will never see all the fruits of her labor, but she will be hailed as one of the pioneers who started the conversation and inspired actions taken for women everywhere.

Stepping In

There is a certain pressure about the arena. There are more eyes on you. People are more critical, and you might not even be sure who's in what seat in the audience…or maybe that keeps changing. Sometimes you don't even realize how heavy the armor is that you're wearing until you step out into the arena, and then you have to deconstruct the fear and worry that are holding you back so that you can be free to do what you are supposed to do.

For example, when it clicked in my mind that day at the Mayo Clinic to hike the Camino to raise money for Dr. Rhodes's study, I had no idea what I was getting myself into. I had no idea if anyone would even consider donating to my cause or if anyone would care about what I was doing. All I knew is that I wanted to hike the Camino and that I was passionate about what Dr. Rhodes was doing. Why not combine the two?

I knew full well that I could end up looking like a fool or end up sending Mayo a dinky check when all was said and done. As I hiked the Camino, I was a little worried about that real possibility. I knew full well that I could end up spending more than a month hiking five hundred miles for something that might hardly make a splash in the study's fundraising needs.

But as I walked, I just kept thinking about what I had learned at Brené Brown's "Daring Way" retreat several years before: to step into the arena, more and more, without any thought of reward or expectations. It was one thing to hike the Camino as a personal pilgrimage, but it was quite another for me to put myself out there and attach it to a cause, welcoming others into that journey with me. I felt a little vulnerable, but I just committed myself to doing what felt right in my soul.

Similarly, writing this book is a continuation of my journey to keep stepping into the arena. There will be criticism, boos from the bleachers, and spitballs from the balcony, all most likely from those who haven't written a book themselves. That's okay; I can handle it. Like many other strong women I know, we are pretty tough when it comes right down to it.

At least in this case, it's certainly worth whatever amount of getting "marred with dust" it takes. There is a story that needs to be told here, and the further I ventured down the Camino road, the more convinced I became that I am someone who should be helping to tell it, no matter whether those in the stands believe I am qualified to do so or not. If I save one life by sharing my story—conveying to women that mammography has been oversold and that there are additional screening technologies that they may need—then it's worth whatever little bit of spitball I may get hit with!

We all have chances in our lives to step into the arena, to go for the gold, no matter how difficult it is, no matter what armor we have worn, or how excited the cheap-seaters are. What is your arena? And what will ultimately get you to step out into it with confidence and boldness?

- 6 -
Signs

"The universe conspires to reveal the truth and to make your path easy if you have the courage to follow the signs."
-Lisa Unger, *New York Times* bestselling author

On the Camino, you find your way by the signs, usually consisting of a large, yellow arrow pointing directly toward the walking path. It's mostly well-marked, except when it isn't. Every now and then, the signs are hidden, mysterious, or even contradictory to one another. They can be down on the ground or on the street curb, up on a post, on the side of a building, or even behind an overgrown tree or bush.

As pilgrims traverse the Camino, the signs can be perfectly clear, missing, confusing, or misleading—which is exactly the way life is.

Also, there are several forks in the road indicating that the Camino goes both ways. Sometimes, this is because people have tampered with the signs as a prank. Other times, it is because there really are two routes that actually connect again in a few miles, though one way might be longer than the other. And then other times, there are big yellow arrows pointing one way but aren't official Camino signs; they have been posted there in an attempt to lead pilgrims to a particular business establishment.

When people encounter these strange and misleading signs, you really start to see various personalities emerge, showing how we each handle confusion and unknowing differently.

There were a few times when I found myself wandering off the official Camino route, but I always eventually found my way back to the main path. Because time wasn't an issue for me, I welcomed the stretches of discovery and meandering. The more I walked, the more I began to welcome the unknowing. Hiking is supposed to be that way. Nature shouldn't have the same clarity and direction as a well-planned trip to Disney World. It should challenge your faith and trust. It should be mysterious.

> *"Before you speak, ask yourself if what you are going to say is true, is it kind, is it necessary, and is it helpful. If the answer is no, maybe what you are about to say should be left unsaid."*

However, what shouldn't feel confusing, misguided, or ill-defined is our walk toward the best breast cancer screening we can get. In this vague and complicated landscape are all kinds of misleading and contradictory signals that, unfortunately, we are left to navigate on our own.

Unlike my walk on the Camino, time is not a luxury when fighting breast cancer. The direction toward the best breast cancer screening for all of us should be obvious without unnecessary confusion, bias, or omission.

Clear Is Kind

Brené Brown, in her best-selling book *Dare to Lead*, talks about the idea that being clear is kind, and being unclear is unkind.

I spent a lot of time on the Camino thinking about this concept (especially whenever I saw an unclear sign that confused pilgrims), what she meant by it, and how I would make a pact with myself to more wholly embody this way of being going forward. I also thought the use of it required some careful consideration.

In the words of the wise radio host Bernard Melzter, "Before you speak, ask yourself if what you are going to say is true, is it kind, is it necessary, and is it helpful. If the answer is no, maybe what you are about to say should be left unsaid."

So, when I'm thinking about saying something that is clear and direct—something that might be difficult for someone else to hear—I run it through Bernard's filter. If it's true, necessary, and helpful, then I will construct my words carefully in order to be clear. And in the case of breast cancer screening, what I've learned—what I now know—is certainly worth being clear about…no matter what.

Unclear Is Unkind

The opposite, then, of being clear to be kind, is being unclear, which turns out to be unkind. Not saying what we really mean, being vague, noncommittal, unresponsive, or engaging in "spin" leaves the receiver of that treatment wondering, left to fill the gaps as they will, and sometimes mistrusting and fearful all together. We've all been on both sides of unclarity, and it really does merit some thinking.

A friend of mine got a letter the other day from her hospital, encouraging her to get her next mammogram, claiming, "Mammograms find the most cancers of any technology." While this is likely true statistically, it is incredibly misleading, especially for women with dense breasts. There are several other ways to actually "find more cancer" than a mammogram in women with dense breasts—and that's many of us!

The statement in that letter is true only because of how long mammography has been around and how widespread it has become. Other technologies that improve the "find rate" of breast cancer over mammography have simply not been around long enough to make such a claim.

So while that statement sounds clear on the surface, it actually sends the wrong message to those of us with dense breasts. It lulls us back into the comfortable belief of thinking that if we get the "all clear" mammogram message, that we definitely don't have breast cancer. Other organizations and imaging societies have made similar statements. Because I do not consider a statement such as this to be the slightest bit clear, I am then left to wonder why they make such a blanket statement when it's not fully true at best, and deceptive at worst. It makes me fearful and distrusting. In other words, it's not clear, and

> *"Not saying what we really mean, being vague, noncommittal, unresponsive, or engaging in 'spin' leaves the receiver of that treatment wondering, left to fill the gaps as they will, and sometimes mistrusting and fearful all together."*

therefore in the end, not kind.

Social media has been helpful in our society for spreading stories, opinions, and creating awareness, but the darker side of marketing is that you can spin just about anything to propagate your own narrative. I have seen Facebook ads from prominent hospitals advertising "peace of mind" for women with dense breast tissue by offering 3D mammography and ultrasound. Of course, I have to comment on the post, "You really aren't offering peace of mind," followed by a statement of verifiable facts to back up my claim, which I know they also have seen. Their statements are misleading at best, and certainly not completely clear given what we now know, so I wholeheartedly believe they are not kind. They aren't offering the very best to patients in ads like this; rather, they are selling what they have.

Spinning the truth is not the truth and makes it all very unclear. What the truth is, at its core, is providing an accurate and holistic picture...and that is largely not what we are getting. Nothing compares to advocating for ourselves in this rocky landscape of misinformation and spin. It is ever more important for us to learn, advocate, and share. We have quite a long way to go before we can say that all signs clearly point in the best direction for women with dense breasts and their breast cancer screening, so that we are the kindest to all. In this case, the kindest result means finding the most breast cancers as early as possible.

But that won't happen until we, as a society, get clear.

Camino de Santiago
Camino francés

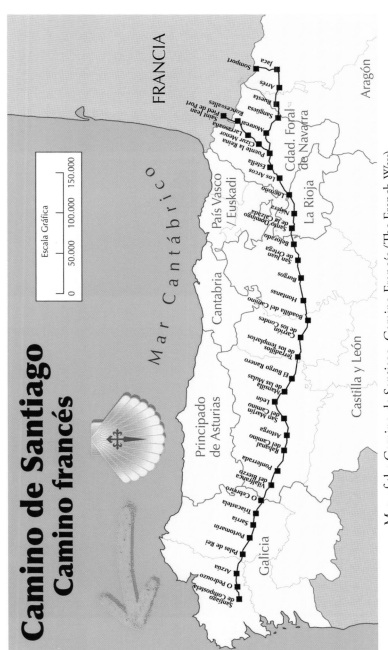

Map of the Camino de Santiago, Camino Francés (The French Way)

St. James the Great

The Pyrenees

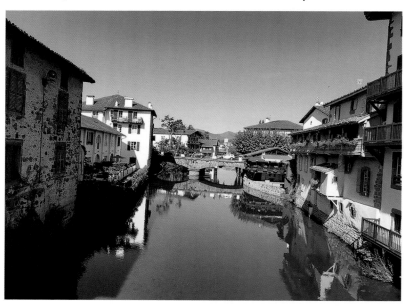

St.- Jean-Pied-de-Port, France

A pilgrim's heart art along the way

Windmills everywhere

A welcome sight in the distance

Confusing signs

Vineyards and hay fields for miles and miles

Rioja wine region

A great resting spot

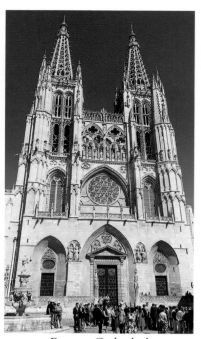

The seemingly endless road on
the Meseta

Burgos Cathedral

St. Nicholas Hospital

Lit candles for five friends who
passed away from breast cancer

Sunrise over the Meseta

The Cathedral Square in Leon

Incredible stained glass in Leon
Cathedral

"The key to the essence is the presence"

An early start sometimes means a beautiful view

The worsening weather at the Cruz de Ferro

One of the tiny churches that are in almost every small town

The Climb to O'Cobriero

Mysterious misty mornings

A *donativo* energy boost for pilgrims

Sharing the Camino with all of God's creatures

My Camino family the night before the finish

A peek at the Santiago Cathedral spires, half a mile away

Minutes before reaching the Cathedral at Santiago de Compostela in Galicia

Seeing the Botafumeiro swing

Camino family celebration

A greeting for passing pilgrims

- 7 -
Donativo

"There are two objects of medical education: to heal the sick, and to advance the science."
-Charles H. Mayo, 1926

*D*onativo, at its most basic level, simply means "donation" in Spanish. On the Camino, however, the word takes on a more complex meaning, best described as "give what you can, and take what you need." It's really more of a philosophy—a way of being—rather than just a simple name or action.

Centuries ago, when people would make the Camino pilgrimage, places that housed pilgrims were called "hospitals." They really weren't medical facilities, although I have to think there was quite a bit of healing going on. I came to understand *donativo* more deeply when I encountered the ancient Ermita de San Nicolás (St. Nicholas Hospital) about halfway through the Camino. It is still open today and operates exactly as it always has, with no facilities, no running water, and no power.

St. Nicholas Hospital still hosts about twelve people a night, and by today's standards, it is very primitive. Dinners and breakfasts are prepared together over an open fire, and the hosts at St. Nicholas wash the pilgrims' feet nightly by candlelight. Legend has it that bats hover around the ceiling once the candles are snuffed out for the evening.

I did not get to stay there, but I did spend some time there because they offer coffee and refreshments to all pilgrims passing by during the day—*donativo*, of course. There is no set charge for refreshments or to stay overnight, and nothing is asked in return for the hospitality.

My guess is that way back when, before the Camino became as commercialized as it is now, most places of refuge for pilgrims operated under *donativo* terms. Back when many pilgrims did not have the resources we have today and were left somewhat at the mercy of anyone willing to help them, pilgrims also would trade goods or offer their labor in trade for food and a night's stay. Or they were simply taken in through the kindness of strangers.

This concept would have been key to the early pilgrims because, at times, the Camino once was a dangerous and treacherous journey. Conversely, the *donativo* model is built on honesty, trust, generosity, and connectivity.

Donativo Multiplied

Currently, there are three basic types of *albergues* (the word "hospital" is no longer used), where the majority of pilgrims stay for the night. Municipal *albergues* are the largest and cheapest and are run by the town in which they are located. Usually no meal is provided at the municipals, but there is most often a kitchen in which you can cook your own food. Privately owned *albergues*, on the other hand, are typically run by their owners and are a little "nicer." They cost a few euros more than the municipals and often offer a pilgrim's menu for dinner in-house or close by.

"It doesn't take much for something that began with pure intentions to be hijacked by money and power, and all of a sudden do the exact opposite of its original intent."

And lastly, parochial *albergues* are run by local Catholic churches and sometimes still operate under *donativo* terms. You can still stay in those for free, if you'd like. No judgment. Nobody is watching. A Pilgrim's Mass is offered to anyone and all who wish to attend. These parochial alternatives are a welcome remnant of the olden days of pilgrim hospitals, such as St. Nicholas. These parochial *albergues* are run by members of the church, an order of nuns, or sometimes volunteers who come in a couple of weeks at a time to help out. The religious system and the people supporting these *albergues* live with a mentality of abundance, as opposed to a scarcity paradigm. They believe that the pilgrims who can't afford it will be covered by someone else who has money to spare, that the pilgrims who don't want to give any money whatsoever to the church will be covered by someone else who is willing and able to give extra, and that the pilgrims who are caught up in a scarcity mentality will be covered by those who live in an abundance mentality. The people who manage the parochial *albergues* operate out of true gratitude for what they have been given and a desire to share what they have with others to support them on their journeys.

The idea of *donativo* stood out to me in radical contrast to the way things operate in today's scorekeeping world. Money, in a scarcity mind-set, is often the underlying cause of stress and conflict as we try to accumulate as much as we need (or more) so that we can show that we are ahead, that we've "won." The hunger for money breaks up friendships, marriages, and families. Greed blocks social progress. It tears apart communities. It wrecks institutions. It creates blind spots and ultimately leads to breakdowns in systems. It doesn't take much for something that began with pure intentions to be hijacked by money and power, and all of a sudden do the exact opposite of its original intent.

But with a *donativo* approach on the Camino, the power of money is dismantled through a trust that those who find refuge in an *albergue* will simply give what they can and take what they need—and this is exactly as it should be. A number of monasteries around the world that offer retreats to their visitors also have this same model.

> *"If more people operated under donativo, what would the world be like? If more people pursued the deep missions on their hearts with little regard for what they got in return or protecting what they already have, what would the world be like?"*

Obviously, it's too idealistic to think that every system or institution can operate this way, but one must wonder: If more people operated under *donativo*, what would the world be like? If more people pursued the deep missions on their hearts with little regard for what they got in return or protecting what they already have, what would the world be like? If more healthcare companies honestly considered what is best for a group collectively rather than what is best for their own quarterly profits or stock prices, what would the world be like?

If institutions, organizations, big businesses, and systems used their existing infrastructure to implement *donativo*, what would the world be like?

A Better Foundation

The most common *albergues* on the Camino are the large, open rooms with rows of adjacent bunk beds. Sleeping in a room with fifty other people is a bit of a shock at first. In America, we lock our doors and arm our security systems at night, and perhaps for good reason. But on the Camino, you find yourself trusting fifty random strangers during the most vulnerable part of your day—while you're sleeping!

Sure, you can choose to stay in a hotel instead, because most towns have them. But Camino enthusiasts recommend that you stay in the *albergues*, and so do I. Why? Because the people are as much a part of the Camino as the path you're walking. Because community is as much a part of the Camino as solitude.

These *albergues* are a little disorienting at first, most noticeably that no one, for the most part, feels the need to protect their belongings. There are no lockers. There are no separate rooms to keep your things. Pilgrims simply check into the *albergues* after a long day of walking, find their beds, leave their belongings on them, shower, and then go out into the town for dinner and drinks. Then, at night, you simply put your belongings under or by your bed while you sleep. In either case, it would be so easy to steal people's things, but no one does. It is extremely rare for that to happen.

I can't say theft has never happened on the Camino (of course it has), but there is a refreshing inherent trust that people have for one another as they all journey to the same place together. Although I admit that the way I describe the Camino can feel a bit utopian at times, it is a glimpse of what we could be as a people if we all came together, united under our common goals and struggles and our shared human nature. I believe it can inspire us to be better.

In America, there is a natural distrust for one another that undermines our way of life. It rises up out of our transactional approach to relationships, along with our fear of scarcity—that feeling that we need to accumulate all we can before someone else does. But the Camino is exactly the opposite. In fact, on the Camino, you want to have as little as possible because you have to carry your belongings in your backpack all day. Therefore, you are motivated to have fewer things—only the items you really need and no more, as if anything additional is a burden to carry. And in fact, it is just that. The environment of the Camino positions pilgrims to start with trust, not with fear; with abundance, and not with scarcity.

There are few things in the States that we fear more than crime. With that fear comes a mental cost—we are so used to worrying about crime that we find ourselves timid in the world and hyper-aware of all that could go wrong…wondering if we remembered to lock the car…or if we engaged the home alarm system…or feeling afraid to walk to our car in a dark parking lot at night. These are all symptoms resulting from our fear. These are all burdens that we unconsciously assimilate, until we get to a place where we no longer need to do that. Then, we notice that we feel differently. Because of the trusting atmosphere, walking the Camino seems like a burden lifted, and you feel as if that lift actually lightens your load.

> *"Whereas the American Dream is built on the cornerstones of safety and security, which often involves shutting others out or using them as stepping stones, the concepts of trust and abundance are all about elevating a different kind of dream—a collective dream, not a selfish dream."*

Although *The Way* is one of my favorite movies, I was sad to go back and watch the trailer and notice that, in a scene in which a young local steals the backpack that belonged to Martin Sheen's character and runs off with it, the Camino was depicted as a dangerous expedition. It hardly is. No more so than traveling anywhere else, and most likely less.

In the Camino guidebook[9] the Irishman gave me, the author, John Brierly, quotes these words from William Arthur Ward's poem, "Risk":

9. Brierley, John. *A Pilgrims Guide to the Camino De Santiago: St. Jean, Roncesvalles, Santiago: the Way of St. James: the Ancient Pilgrim Path Also Known as Camino Francés: a Practical & Mystical Manual for the Modern-Day Pilgrim.* Forres: Camino Guides, 2017.

But risks must be taken
Because the greatest hazard in life is to risk nothing.
The people who risk nothing may avoid suffering and sorrow,
But they cannot learn, feel, change, grow or really live.
Chained by their servitude they are slaves who have forfeited
all freedom.
Only a person who risks is truly free.

I believe that trusting in those around us and/or in a divine power frees us up to unlock something within ourselves that we didn't know we had. It allows us to take risks that we might not have ever fathomed taking. It frees us up to take risks because we believe that life, despite its darkness, is inherently good and that people, despite their flaws, are inherently all on the same team. Whereas the American Dream is built on the cornerstones of safety and security, which often involves shutting others out or using them as stepping stones, the concepts of trust and abundance are all about elevating a different kind of dream—a collective dream, not a selfish dream.

On the Camino, the notions of protecting what you have at all costs, and accumulating all you can, is completely abandoned. You simply follow the path forward and trust your fellow pilgrims along the way. You stop worrying about yourself or your "stuff," and you start to see life through a more collective lens. When you have trust, what is there to fear? Instead of a me-centered approach to your life, your mentality is naturally reframed to an us-centered approach. You begin to feel free. You begin to feel more connected to those around you.

How can we get the breast-cancer-screening world to take the risk, to reconnect to women collectively, and to trust that finding the most breast cancers as early as possible is the main priority so that the ultimate prize is that more women with breast cancer become survivors? This might mean disregarding who makes the most money, sells the most equipment, or performs the most biopsies. Can we unite around elevating the health of women above all else?

Donativo would be an especially profound posture in the worlds of medicine and healthcare, which largely has been hijacked by big business and greed. Major decisions are made by insurance companies and large corporations with the financial means to market what they are selling, not necessarily what is best for the good of the whole.

So much of our mistrust in healthcare and medicine today ultimately stems from a scarcity mentality—that desire to win, that need to be profitable, possibly at the expense of those who are supposed to be served. Individuals and organizations are caught up in selfish motives and continue to make decisions that are money-focused rather than patient-focused—quite the opposite of *donativo*.

A Modern-Day St. Nicholas Hospital

In September 2018, PBS released a documentary that was produced and directed by Ken Burns titled *The Mayo Clinic: Faith–Hope–Science*, which tells the incredible story of the Mayo Clinic's origins and how its values are still just as inspiring today. I highly recommend watching it.

The documentary, which includes interviews with the Dalai Lama and the late John McCain, provides a stark contrast to today's broken healthcare system, which has become too motivated by financial incentives and ego. It does this subtly through factual storytelling by simply showing how, from its inception, the Mayo Clinic has approached healthcare in an otherworldly, generous, non-transactional, more "*donativo*" way.

The Mayo Clinic is not perfect. I believe they must struggle daily to stay true to their origin and to always focus on the patient first in a world where our healthcare systems are anything but that, where insurance companies, not patients with their physicians, often dictate how we'll be treated, and where drug costs are skyrocketing. Nonetheless, I must say I do notice a difference when I am there. I can feel the impact of this different mentality, this different way of being that they manage to embody. It is refreshing to say the least.

This difference that many people feel stems all the way back to the early days of the clinic, when the Mayo family, with the help of the nearby Sisters of Saint Francis in Rochester, Minnesota, continually lived out of a profound sense of trust that things would work out if their hearts were in the right place—if they made decisions out of their connection to their patients and those whom they believed they were called to serve, rather than worrying about finances or thriving as a business. An early example of this is the founder, W. W. Mayo, and his wife, Louise, mortgaging their home in 1869 to buy a new, expensive microscope that would help them serve their patients better.

To this day, doctors at the Mayo Clinic are on salary, with no compensation given or taken related to the number of people they see, the number of tests they order, or any other activity that either generates revenue or saves costs. This frees them up to do the right thing for patients without monetary factors clouding their judgment.

John McCain had a great quote in the documentary: "Doctors that are at the very top of their profession, they could be anywhere and yet they've decided to stay with Mayo. There are people there who could be making ten times the amount of money that they're making at Mayo, but they are devoted to their profession and their science of medicine and healing people." This is closer to the *donativo* way of being, and I believe this is a major reason why the Mayo Clinic continually is ranked as the number one hospital in the United States and in many disciplines within the medical field. Almost every Mayo doctor conducts research of some kind, also making them truly cutting-edge in many areas of research.

I also believe that this environment enabled doctors and scientists there to see a big hole in the breast-cancer-screening system. Too many breast cancers are not visible in women with dense breasts via the current technologies used. Mayo Clinic doctors aim to create a solution to that problem— not to profit for themselves, but for the good of the whole—because it is in the best interest of their patients and women everywhere. Quite conversely, in the end, if and when we begin to find more and more breast cancers earlier, when treatment and surgery are less extensive and therefore less expensive, *less* money will likely be generated from treating those cancers, not *more*.

Early detection not only saves more lives; it's a lot less costly in the aggregate and over the long run. Take it from somebody living with Stage 4 breast cancer—it's expensive! Yet the pushback from the industry as a whole has been huge in getting this technology out into the public, where it can do the most good. Everyone has their stated reason, or excuse. That all leaves me wondering, mistrustful, and left to surmise what is really going on at the peril of women everywhere.

The Mayo Clinic, as its standard, now screens all dense-breast patients with MBI every other year, alternating with 3D mammography in an effort to find breast cancer early for those women with dense breasts, whose success with standard mammography has proven to be limited. Why don't we all have access to that? Or if not MBI exactly, then something comparable?

Just as the parochial *albergues* on the Camino practice *donativo* in order to prioritize people's transformation on their pilgrimage, Mayo has historically done the same in serving their patients and making people's health the most important priority. On the Camino, the worldly scheme of money takes a backseat to people's spiritual journeys and their psychological healing from whatever burdens they are carrying. Similarly, Mayo is using its resources and infrastructure not to make the most money, but rather to elevate people's souls and inner journeys: their mental and emotional health.

Yes, corporations have a bottom line to watch. And yes, CEOs really are compensated by short-term gains and rising stock prices. And yes, the harsh reality is that much of medicine is actually physician-focused, not patient-focused. But I believe William James Mayo, the son of W. W. Mayo, said it best nearly a century ago: "The greatest asset of a nation is the health of its people. The medical profession can be the greatest factor for good in America. Our failures as a profession are the failures of individualism, the result of competitive medicine. It must be done by collective effort." Those words could not be more relevant today, and clearly the progress in breast-cancer screening has suffered from the results of competitive medicine that W. W. Mayo spoke about.

So how do we speed up the advancement of the next generation of breast cancer screening for the collective health of our daughters, friends, mothers, sisters, coworkers, and ourselves, so that more women with breast cancer become survivors? It starts with us advocating for ourselves and for our family members and friends. It starts with women *and* doctors holding the old mammography story just a little more loosely, and it starts with providers thinking beyond the bottom line, about what's right and good for all. It starts with honesty, trust, and integrity. On our journey to better breast care for all, there is going to have be more *donativo*-based decision making along the way from all of us.

What part of *donativo* are you willing to embrace?

- 8 -
The Meseta

*"What if you bowed before every dandelion you met and wrote
love letters to squirrels and pigeons who crossed your path? What
if scrubbing the dishes became an act of single reverence for the
gift of being washed clean, and what if the rhythmic percussion
of chopping carrots became the drumbeat of your dance? What
if you stepped into the shower each morning only to be baptized
anew and sent forth to serve the grocery bagger, the bank teller,
and the bus driver through simple kindness? And what if the things
that make your heart dizzy with delight were no longer stuffed into
the basement of your being and allowed out to play in the lush and
green fields? There are two ways to live in this world: as if everything
were enchanted or nothing at all."*
-Christine Valters Paintner, *The Soul of a Pilgrim*

The second third of the Camino is known as the "mental" aspect
of the journey because you traverse the Meseta, meaning the high
plains, or plateau, in the north-central part of Spain between Burgos
and Leon, for about 112 miles.

Physically, it becomes easier because the terrain has flattened consid-
erably after the breathtaking mountains of the Pyrenees and the scenic
rolling hills of the Rioja wine region. However, the Meseta is known
as the mental portion because, quite frankly, there is a lot less to look
at. The lush green animal pastures and the picturesque vineyards of the
first third of the Camino give way to flatlands—field after field of hay

and corn, with some sunflowers thrown in, if you are lucky. It's what I would imagine Kansas might be like to walk across.

What's so "mental" about it is that there is much less distraction, leaving more time to think while you walk, and walk while you think, repeated over and over again for twelve to fourteen days. Most pilgrims would say that this is where physical struggles start to fade and the inner work begins, where old burdens are laid to rest, leaving room for something new and true to grow.

Although there are a few interesting towns on the Meseta, many nights are spent in tiny towns that, without the pilgrims, would be completely abandoned and left to ruin. Some contain only one *albergue*, maybe one bar, perhaps a very small store, and a church that is often no longer operating and locked. You are left to wonder who once lived in these towns, why they left, where they went, who tends the crops, and what it means exactly that all the churches are locked so you can't get in.

Along the second third of the journey, the undulation of your daily hikes significantly decreases, but the length often increases. There are very few trees, so shade becomes scarce. The Meseta is particularly harsh in the summer, reaching temperatures of well over 100 degrees. Your walk begins to feel nomadic as you wander, day after day, through flat farmland as far as the eye can see in every direction. It is as if you are hiking through a desert. It is so monotonous, in fact, that some people take a taxi or a bus to bypass this part, or they rent a bicycle to quicken the trip, returning it at Leon or Astorga, where the terrain starts to get hillier once again. This is completely understandable, but in my opinion, to skip the Meseta—the mental part of the journey—is to miss one of the most important parts of all.

The Beauty Behind You

A fellow pilgrim commented to me as we entered the Meseta, "The sunrises during this leg are the most beautiful of the entire Camino, but you have to remember to turn around and look behind you to see them." Of course, this is actually true. The trail points due west to Santiago, so we had to stop and turn around to see the sunrises. And beautiful they were, with vivid pink, purple, and gold colors.

This also made for a great metaphor, prompting me to take the time to stop and appreciate where I had come from. I thought a lot about what a great family I have, how much I love my husband and kids, and how lucky I have been to have lived the life I have had. I have traveled to unique places, have many good friends and neighbors and fellow parishioners at my church, and I want for nothing. I decided somewhere out there in those massive fields that the gratitude I was feeling felt so good that I wanted to keep it up. I vowed to make a habit of gratitude.

Those vast flatlands with endless hay and corn I was walking through also reminded me of my childhood home in southern Indiana. I grew up in a little town called Worthington, which honestly feels just like the Meseta. There never really was much exciting going on, though I loved growing up there. I knew no different. Hiking the Meseta—with its big, open fields, the occasional animal smells, barns, silos, and farm equipment—came with the feeling that I had the world to myself, and it was strangely nostalgic for me. Even though I had never been to that particular area in Spain before, it felt a little like home, and that gave me a sense of peace.

It is appropriate as well to stop and take an appreciative look at how far we really have come with breast cancer screening as treatment and care in general, lest we get too wrapped up in being upset about the current state of affairs. Although there is no doubt I am calling for more advances, it is important to realize that in the 1960s, the annual death rate from breast cancer was around 72,000 women per year in the United States. Because of mammography and better cancer treatment, that number has come down to around 41,000 per year.

Many people in the medical field, as well as advocacy groups, have dedicated themselves to public awareness, improved chemotherapy, endocrine therapies, and new surgical techniques. We've come a long way, and thanks to those advances, many kids still have their moms and grandmothers, husbands still have their wives, and people still have their sisters, friends, and coworkers. There is still a lot of work to do, but very thankfully, much progress has been made.

Presence and Positivity

During particularly long stretches between towns seemingly in the middle of nowhere, there would sometimes be a very welcome temporary rest area, with drinks and food, a hammock to lie in, a blanket to sit on, or other forms of creature comforts available for pilgrims—

donativo style, of course.

Those comforts were always perfectly placed, as if the universe knew exactly when and how pilgrims needed to rest and refresh. These things always had sort of a Zen about them, and I nicknamed them "hippy hangouts." They were among my favorite spots. I stayed a while at each one and hated to leave when it was time to hit the trail again. At one such place, the owner had painted the front of his food stand with the phrase, "The key of the essence is the presence." So true.

Indeed, the flatlands of the Meseta can teach you much, should you decide to learn from them.

"If we are focused on the destination and are allowing ourselves to get discouraged on a daily basis because we aren't where we want to be, then it's unlikely that we will find the beauty in the process."

First, through the monotony and unchanging views, I began to think about the idea that life really isn't exciting all of the time, just like the Meseta portion of the Camino isn't all that exciting to look at, especially after a few days. There will be really eventful times in life, with some doldrums in between. There is work, chores, and many other things in life that must be done but that aren't particularly new or even fun. However, the Meseta showed me that you can enjoy whatever is there, if you choose to. During my time walking these flats, I made a pact with myself to slow down enough to enjoy whatever I was doing, wherever I was doing it. I will enjoy the essence by being present.

Having so much time and space to only walk and think, I also came to understand that we get to dictate our own reality with the power of our own thoughts. No matter how challenging or overwhelming or grim our life situations might be, we get to determine whether we will accept either a victim narrative or a narrative that empowers us to carry on with conviction and purpose. As related to flatlands themselves, you realize that you can either accept whatever landscape you are in and find the beauty in it, or you can complain about it, stagger through it, or even bypass it altogether. As Ralph Waldo Emerson said, "You are what you think all day long."

If we are focused on how miserable, monotonous, or boring things are, then we are probably not going to be thinking about turning around to see the splendor of a sunrise, and we will miss it altogether. If we are focused on the *destination* and are allowing ourselves to get discouraged on a daily basis because we aren't where we want to be, then it's unlikely that we will find the beauty in the *process*. The more positive we are, the better it is for our health. Since my body has been infected by something I cannot control (cancer), I believe that I need to do everything I can to affect it positively. That means taking the time to look at sunsets and enjoying the process as I live out the rest of my days.

And finally, as I walked the long days of the Meseta, what I felt called to do with the next phase of my life began to solidify in my mind. It started to feel more and more right for me to share my story in hopes that it would help other women and nudge us closer to the next generation of breast cancer screening. It was still quite unclear exactly how that would play out, what it would look like, and exactly how I would do it, but I was beginning to have confidence that those details would come to light.

With all that time to think and process my life and its direction, I was becoming more and more convinced that I was on the right path—that breast cancer screening is the avenue in which I should focus my energy and resources, and through that, give back to the world. The Camino was bringing me into deeper contact with my purpose.

Great Things Ahead

After many days on the Meseta, pilgrims finally reach the city of Leon, which is a welcome change, with its impressive towering cathedral, plentiful restaurants, and bustling shops. Most people take a day off from walking to enjoy the city, visit the cathedral, and just be tourists for a day.

At this point, the plateau of the Meseta is behind you, and there is prettier (though more challenging) terrain ahead, on your way to Santiago. This is something to look forward to after conquering the "mental" third of the Camino.

Metaphorically speaking, after a long stretch of flats, but before another landscape change, is where I see our current state of affairs with breast cancer screening. In fact, we've been stuck right outside "Leon" for a long time. For quite a while, we've been doing the same thing over and over, using the same technologies with very little change, producing more or less the same results. If you were to look at a graph of annual deaths from breast cancer over the past fifty years, you would see what looks like a hill that drops dramatically and has now flattened out.

We have plateaued and have stayed there for many years. For more than a decade, we've known that breast density masks cancers on mammograms, but we've actually done very little about it. So on the plateau we stay, seemingly lulled into thinking that this plateau we are on is all there is. But it's not, and we need to start the next leg of the breast-cancer-screening journey.

> "With the advent of Molecular Breast Imaging and possibly some other new modalities as well, we are poised to make moves that get us to a better place, where more cancers can be found earlier, when they are curable."

Quite simply stated, it's now time to move off the plateau, because we can. And if we can, then we must. With the advent of Molecular Breast Imaging and possibly some other new modalities as well, we are poised to make moves that get us to a better place, where more cancers can be found earlier, when they are curable. Some people will be dragged, kicking and screaming, off the plateau. Others might elect to stay behind while the rest of the world moves on. But just like most other large-scale changes, a few early adopters will lead the way toward the next generation of breast cancer screening, and then most everyone else will either willingly or begrudgingly follow. It might be a pretty bumpy road as companies compete for new equipment sales, providers might disagree about what to or not to do, and medical boards will probably differ in opinion, perhaps putting up roadblocks to slow down progress.

But in the end, it is intolerable to stay on the plateau forever, and we must continue the journey onward to provide better screening for women everywhere. It is time for all of us to accept this reality.

- 9 -
Acclimation

*"Yes, transformation is often more about unlearning than
learning, which is why the religious traditions call it 'conversion' or
'repentance.'"*
-Richard Rohr, *Falling Upward*

O ne of the many interesting things about the Camino is that you
adapt to its varying climate and imperfections, and those new
things can become part of what you like about it. Because you are
thrown into a new environment and culture with no real escape (unless
you quit and go home), this acclimation actually happens very quickly.

One might think that while hiking the Meseta in the blistering heat,
for example, everyone would flood into an air-conditioned bar as soon
as possible upon reaching the next town. Well, they do, but then they
grab their drink or food and almost always go right back outside. It
feels weird and wrong to stay inside too long. Even if it's hot or muggy,
pilgrims generally prefer to remain outside. Even when it's raining,
many will still go out.

The same thing happens with the sleeping arrangements in the
albergues. You might think you could never get used to sleeping in a
huge room, on a thin twin bed, with fifty other people, right next to a
stranger. But the few times I stayed in a hotel, while I did enjoy aspects
of it, I actually felt a little lonely. I missed the camaraderie of my fellow

pilgrims. I had gotten used to having so many other people around, even if I didn't know each one personally.

Why does this happen? Perhaps it's because we humans really are just higher-order animals after all and are meant to be outdoors a lot more than our modern-day society allows. Maybe it's because we actually are a herd species, meant to be in community with each other, thriving better together than apart. Or maybe we simply have the ability to acclimate to our surroundings merely as a means of survival. Regardless of the reasons, how we quickly acclimate is very apparent on the Camino. The outdoors, no matter the weather, just becomes a part of you because you spend most of your time each day outside. You accept whatever climate comes your way and thrive within it.

As I neared the end of the Meseta, I became concerned that I wasn't going to reach Leon in time, where I needed to take a blood test at their hospital so that they could send the results to my doctors by a certain date. To meet the deadline, I unfortunately had to take a cab for ten or fifteen miles one day so I could get to Leon. Although I didn't have a choice, it felt weird sitting inside a cab and moving quickly through the countryside. It felt wrong. Not because it felt like I was cheating. It just felt foreign. I wanted to get outside again; I felt a bit trapped. In the indoors, you have more control over your environment, but in the outdoors, you have an opportunity to partner with something as magnificent and all powerful as the climate.

What I came to understand on the Camino, especially in the monotony of the flatlands, was that the weather was a wave you were supposed to ride, enriching the experience. Whether dark storm clouds rolled across the plains or the skies were a crystal-clear blue, it was as if each varying pattern of the skies beckoned you to gaze upon it, savor it, and fully experience whatever it had to offer.

The weather, in fact, broke up the monotony of the Meseta. I noticed more about the weather during that period of the journey than I ever had in my entire life because of the expanse of the skies in that flat space. I could see a weather change coming from the distant horizon, and it was usually a welcome change. To experience whatever it was I was supposed to experience in any present moment was an enlightening way to learn to accept what is, enjoy it, make friends with it, and acclimate to the journey.

New Normal

When you spend a long amount of time outside, you start to see your body's relationship with the weather, and you kind of become one with it.

Like a farmer who depends on the weather, you begin to develop a relationship with the natural world. Sometimes it is absolutely glorious, and sometimes it beats you down. Either way, you realize that it's just the way things are—that the perfection, heat, cold, rain, or dryness all have something unique to offer for your benefit. Even if it's incredibly uncomfortable, you realize that you still get to decide how you react to it. You can either begrudge it or embrace it.

While I was walking all those miles, I came to view my acceptance of the cancer diagnosis as being quite like acclimating to the natural environment on the Camino. Although each person must do his or her own inner work through grief, loss, and acceptance, I have come to view cancer like the weather. It's just there, and I can't really change it, and in my case, there is no getting rid of it. Given that reality, some sort of peaceful coexistence must take place between it and me. Even a sort of synergy, perhaps.

"Some have made the mistake of calling me 'sick.' I'm not sick. I can only be 'sick' if I believe I'm sick. Sick is a perspective you adopt."

This is why I am not fond of the term "fighting" or "battling" cancer. Rather, I prefer to think of it more as a relationship. Cancer is part of me, and I am its chosen host. It is simply now a part of my natural life bringing its own mountains and valleys, sunny skies, and potentially violent storms. Like the scorching heat or cascading rainfalls on the Camino, it is something I believe I am supposed to walk with—to carry it with me, yet move forward regardless, step after step, even amid possible discomfort. It is a wave that has asked me to ride it.

Some have made the mistake of calling me "sick." I'm not sick. I can only be "sick" if I believe I'm sick. Sick is a perspective you adopt. Others have told me that I should stop working so hard and to simply rest and relax. You know, because I have cancer. Though I know they mean well, it's almost as if they are telling me to throw in the towel just because of the intensity of my diagnosis. Problems come into our lives all the time. We fight them and rise above them. Why is it that when it comes to cancer, we all seem to slip into the grip of fear? I decided to acknowledge my fear. And sometimes that means confronting it.

"There's no changing the weather, just like there's no changing my story. But I can acclimate to it and use it as a unique opportunity to help others by sharing what I have learned through my own story, journey, and walk through life."

To this point, although I really am upbeat most of the time, I do have my moments, and sometimes they come most unexpectedly. Not long ago, a trusted journalist asked me to put my fear into words so we could connect more deeply with the audience the story was for. Much to my surprise, I started crying. The sudden wave of emotion caught me off guard. We were in a noisy coffee shop, and I was sitting there crying. Those are the times when some inner truth seeps out. I'm no longer afraid of these kinds of emotions.

Moreover, I sometimes become saddened when I think about being unable to be the steady foundation for my children that I've always tried to be for them, or not having the opportunity to be a grandmother, as my own grandma had a massive impact on my own life, or not getting everything done that I want to get done around breast cancer screening. But all this, like the weather, is beyond my control.

This acceptance certainly has taken me a while to get to. For the first six months or so after my diagnosis, I really didn't want most people to know. Because I didn't look, act, or feel any different, that was pretty easy to get by with. It took me time to acclimate. What I've found is that as uncomfortable as my storm was at first, now it is something I embrace. It is my new normal. If I could go back and rewrite my story, I certainly wouldn't include Stage 4 cancer. But given the reality of it, I am going to do my best in the climate I find myself in.

There's no changing the weather, just like there's no changing my story. But I can acclimate to it and use it as a unique opportunity to help others by sharing what I have learned through my own story, journey, and walk through life.

Reacclimating

Like the weather on the Camino, nothing in life ever stays the same.

It is rightly said that the only constant we really have is change. Therefore, resisting, or not acclimating, in the end, only makes things worse.

Had I been resistant to accepting my new normal upon being diagnosed with Stage 4 breast cancer, I would not have had the pleasure of walking the Camino or meeting so many wonderful people along the way. Similarly, had I failed to embrace the Camino as is, I might have missed out on a lot of those colorful sunrises, the shades of the different fields of crops reminiscent of my Indiana childhood, the magnificence of those roaming livestock, and the overall beauty of northern Spain.

Over the past few decades, the medical community and advocacy groups have certainly acclimated to mammography as the "gold standard" for breast cancer screening (though even today, there is still disagreement regarding at what age women should get their first mammogram). Actually, they have acclimated so well that they are now stuck. Apparently, the current climate has gotten very comfortable.

There has, however, been a different weather pattern on the horizon for a while now, something that will alter the breast-cancer-screening landscape permanently. Science and technology have revealed to us just how pivotal breast density is in getting the right screening.

For more than a decade, we have known that dense breast tissue masks cancer on mammogram images. Lots of work has been done by many, but in spite of all of that, there has been resistance, and quite a bit of it. The path ahead is clearly leading us toward the horizon, farther into the unknown. But most would rather stay right where they are instead of reacclimating to whatever we encounter as we move toward our destination.

People have acclimated well to mammography. Now it's time to keep marching forward and reacclimate to Molecular Breast Imaging and other breast-imaging technologies that will be transformative for women with dense breasts. And, if people aren't moving forward, as they haven't been for a while now, then maybe we can accelerate that weather pattern on the horizon by raising awareness about breast density and supplemental screening options, by speaking up and demanding the right care from physicians.

If those who are calling the shots aren't going to move toward the destination and reacclimate to life-saving science and technology, then maybe it's time for us to rain down on them.

Because you are reading this book, there is a good chance you've been impacted by cancer in some way. If you don't know anyone who has had their life rocked by cancer, then there is a good chance that somewhere in the back of your mind, you fear the possibility of getting cancer yourself. Instead of fearing cancer, let's partner with it. Let's allow cancer to be an invitation to advocacy, thereby inviting the rain and forcing a new climate where all women with dense breast tissue can get a screening that detects a lot more of their cancer.

To be sure, some parts of the medical community have already acclimated; they are ready for what is to come and likely welcome it. Others will refuse to see that the rain is coming and will be completely blindsided when it hits them. Nonetheless, this change, like the weather on the Meseta in Spain, will occur no matter what, and all will have to acclimate eventually. The faster the better, and the sooner the easier.

How can you take the next step in the process of your life by first acclimating to your present situation?

- 10 -
Declaration

"He who is doing his true will is assisted by the momentum of the universe."
-Peter J. Carroll

I finally arrived in Leon after twelve days on the Meseta. I spent three days there, mostly being a tourist among friends but also getting a blood test (which turned out just fine). I once again headed out on foot westward toward Astorga—approximately the last third of the journey to Santiago. I was refreshed, ready, and definitely felt like I had gained momentum—a common feeling for pilgrims who experience the excitement of Leon after hiking through farmland for so long.

About 102 miles ahead, pilgrims finally begin to make their last big climb up to a town called O'Cobriero before descending into the region of Galicia and Santiago. I was looking forward to it and felt ready for the challenge. By this time, having passed the halfway point and completing most of the flatlands, walking felt easier, and my body felt stronger. Physically, I felt like I had gotten into the groove.

However, a lingering thought on my mind heading into the final stretch had to do with fundraising. I mentioned earlier how vulnerable it felt to attach my pilgrimage to a cause; I was two-thirds of the way done with the walk but had raised only a little more than half of my targeted amount. I was wrestling with accepting that my fundraising goal might not be met. But, as I had vowed in the Meseta, I was finding gratitude in the process anyway, even knowing that I might fall short of my total dollar goal.

Backstory

Just as I had done cardio workouts and strength training that prepared me for the physical demands of the Camino, I had completed a lot of fundraising prep work as well. With a friend and breast cancer survivor, we developed a website (www.walkthewaywithher.com) that explained both Molecular Breast Imaging and goals of the Density MATTERS study.

The site also offered information we thought people would want to know about me, as well as the Camino de Santiago itself. We also developed a donation page that linked directly to the Mayo Clinic website, ensuring that all money went directly to the study. Unlike so many other cancer organizations that raise funds, I was adamant that 100 percent of every donated dollar went directly to the cause. Not creating my own not-for-profit entity or using some other intermediary and going straight to a Mayo Clinic landing page instead ensured that every dollar would be fully used for the Density MATTERS study.

Fundraising was a huge aspect of "stepping out into the arena" for me. It was one thing to hike the Camino and yet another for me to stick my neck way out there and try to raise what seemed to me a huge amount of money. But it put even more purpose behind my walk, which was already deeply personal.

And as the universe would have it, a friend introduced me to Bob Lee, now my good friend and mentor. Bob had ridden his bike all the way around the perimeter of the United States in three segments, raising more than $1 million for three different causes. He is also a pro at creating awareness in the local public for other people trying to do good things. I felt so fortunate to be able to tap into his amazing energy and expertise.

Bob has many talents, and one of his finest skills is that he is an incredible connector of people. Accordingly, he introduced me to Vince Foglia of the Foglia Family Foundation, a generous donor to many charities, both locally and nationally. Bob had recommended that I ask Vince for a $50,000 matching donation; if I raised $50,000 on my own, then Vince would match every dollar up to $50,000.

Never having done anything like that before, I felt uneasy about asking for that much money. But I trusted Bob, and I sensed he was giving me great advice, so I decided to jump in and have faith in what was happening.

When I decided to step out into the arena and put a fundraising purpose behind my pilgrimage, never in my wildest dreams did I imagine I'd be aiming to raise $100,000. It seemed absurd at the time. But as is the nature of the arena, sometimes we just have to keep letting others who are on our team push us forward in unexpected ways. Vince's willingness to join my mission gave a huge boost to my efforts, both incentivizing donors and challenging me to achieve $50,000 on my own to get $100,000 total. It also added some pressure, but there was no turning back! I am ever grateful to both Bob and Vince for their kind generosity in time and money, words of encouragement, and continued support.

All this previous work and support from so many people fueled me while I was walking every day to post at least once a day to Facebook, Instagram, and Twitter, which many people seemed to enjoy. Also, every three or four days, I would take a deeper dive into the intricacies and emotions evoked on the Camino and write a blog about those. As it turned out, many people enjoyed those blogs much more than I realized at the time, often sharing them with family and friends. I think those posts and blogs that people were seeing regularly did encourage some to donate who might not have otherwise.

By the time I was two-thirds of the way done with the Camino, I had raised only $28,000, just a little more than half of the $50,000 I needed to secure all of Vince's additional $50,000 matching gift. On one hand, I was grateful and humbled that people following my journey from the States and even around the world were willing to give as much as they had given. On the other hand, however, I really wanted to reach the goal so that, with Vince's match, the total amount would reach $100,000. I really wanted to do everything I could to move Density MATTERS forward.

Staying in the Arena

Though I was admittedly a bit discouraged that I was not on pace to hit my $50,000 goal when I began the final leg of the Camino, I was also reminded of the nature of the arena. The arena asks us to stay in it, without any thought of reward. It asks us to make our home there, even when our expectations are not being met or when things are not going as well as we might like them to. I decided that what mattered most was that I was putting forth my maximum effort. That was all I could control.

> "When we have the courage to go out into the arena, there is really no such thing as failure. In daring to unleash what is on our hearts, we are already living in a way that the majority of people, who are blinded by comfort and security, are not."

I continued to blog during that final leg, I continued to put myself out there, and I continued to trust in the process. I was determined to finish what I had started. If I did not hit my goal and secure all of Vince's additional $50,000, then so be it. Although that was a difficult thing to accept, it also felt liberating. I decided that under no circumstances would I allow the pilgrimage to be viewed as a failure in any way. Consequently, I think that so much of the arena requires subtle reframing in one's mentality.

When I trained for a marathon many years back, I was committed to simply finishing the marathon. I deliberately avoided focusing on a specific time in which I wanted to finish. I thought, "Why would I open the door for discouragement with the binary labels of 'success' or 'failure' when I am brand new to long-distance running?

This situation was similar. The arena has its demands because of the passions that reside in our hearts, but it also has grace. I had never hiked the Camino before, I had never fundraised before, and I had never been an advocate for breast cancer screening before. So why would I judge myself?

The challenge of the arena is that we declare that we will stay in it, over and over again, without judging ourselves through the lens of expectations or results. Sometimes it is tempting to go up into the cheap seats ourselves and judge our efforts, because we are often our own worst critics. But what's the point of doing that? It just leads to discouragement. Declaring that we will stay in the arena—on the playing surface—and keep giving our all, on the other hand, can inspire growth and grace.

Momentum

As I hiked the final leg, continued blogging, and remained active on social media—updating people who were interested in my journey with my progress—the donations coming in began to pick up pace.

I knew that because once a week, Molly from the Mayo Clinic Development Department would send me updates with a list of donors and the total raised to date so that I could keep tabs on what was going on and thank all the donors properly. (Much of the time I spent in Leon, in fact, was writing "thank you" postcards.) Due to donor privacy laws, the amount every individual gave was not disclosed, but I could see the total number of donors, as well as the total dollar amount growing. I felt so encouraged by the progress I was seeing.

I'm not sure if it was because people had held off donating until I neared the end of my journey, but hardly a day went by during that final leg where something didn't come in. Most were not large donations; they were smaller donations from people showing their support to me, with a few larger ones sprinkled in. All were equally appreciated! With around ten days to go, I was close to the $37,000 mark—still far from reaching my $50,000 goal, but gaining momentum nonetheless.

And that was when the floodgates opened.

With four or five days remaining in the hike, I reached $47,000 and was confident that it would be no problem getting to the $50,000 threshold to ultimately secure Vince's generous $50,000 matching pledge by the time I returned to the States. Thanks to Bob, Vince, and all the incredibly generous people who caught the vision of the Mayo Clinic's groundbreaking work in breast cancer screening and the purpose of my pilgrimage, I was confident we would reach the goal.

Sometimes when we step out into the arena, we reach our goals, and other times, we don't. What's most important is that we keep trying so that we give our goals a chance to be realized. Many people feel the weight of their goals and dreams and never put them into motion because they are afraid of failure, because of the armor they are wearing. But when we have the courage to go out into the arena, there is really no such thing as failure. In daring to unleash what is on our hearts, we are already living in a way that the majority of people, who are blinded by comfort and security, are not.

What really counts is that we keep stepping into the arena. And more often than not, when we disregard the critics in the cheap seats, silence our own judgmental whispers, and are willing to have our faces marred with dust, we are surprised to see the fruit of our efforts, allowing us to achieve what we've always desired.

- 11 -
Spiritual Energy

*"The cosmos is within us. We are made of star-stuff. We are a way for
the universe to know itself."*
-Carl Sagan

M ost obviously, the final third of the Camino is considered
the "spiritual" leg of the journey because people are nearing
the journey's crescendo at the Cathedral at Santiago de Compostela
in Galicia. That is the beautiful, eight-hundred-year-old cathedral
containing the bones of St. James in its catacombs, where every route
of the Camino leads. But for me, what made it "spiritual" is more difficult to describe.

In some ways, the final third of the Camino feels like the first third,
with more hills and less flatlands. Overhanging trees provide shade, and
there are more towns to explore in the evenings, with shorter distances
between them. Because of this change in terrain, scenery, and popula-
tion following the sparseness and monotony of the Meseta, one begins
to sense the energy and collective momentum as pilgrims venture ever
closer to Santiago. Brand-new pilgrims join the journey, while others
are reunited with those they met hundreds of miles back. It feels like a
big family reunion, where some people already know each other, while
others are joining the family for the first time.

It feels magical.

For most pilgrims at this point, any remaining physical aches and pains have subsided and have been replaced by an excitement, a buzz, about reaching the end. My confidence increased as I realized that, barring a major accident, I was actually going to make it! The burdens and baggage I had been carrying seemed a little lighter, my head was clearer, and my mind was more open to wider possibilities. I also knew that my fellow pilgrims had been on a similar journey and that the demands of their unique Camino experience had also inevitably transformed each of them in some way for the better. There was an inherently understood notion of transformation among pilgrims on the trail that created a bond that largely remained unspoken, yet nonetheless was incredibly strong.

This energy intensified even more when I was two or three days out from Galicia because of the sheer number of people filling up the path. I began to see a lot more strangers; many of the people on the path were doing a one-, two-, or three-day walk into Galicia. I found myself just as thankful for the people getting a taste of the Camino, like my husband and I had done the year before, as I was for those who had walked all the way from Saint-Jean-Pied-de-Port, France. It didn't matter how much or how little each person had hiked, what their story was, or why they had been drawn to the Camino. We were all on the path together, venturing to the same place. Each person had his or her own reasons for being on the journey, and that was a good thing. But no matter our differences, we were all pilgrims.

With that said, though, there were certain people, starting from as far back as Pamplona whom I continually found myself walking with, resting with, bunking with, and eating with, right from the very beginning. We often seemed to be in the same place at the same time, having started walking on the same day, and had grown to love each other's company. I knew that must mean something.

About a week before we were to reach Santiago, right around when donations had increased significantly, we decided that it just felt right to enjoy the last few days of the journey together as a "Camino Family." There was Katharina (Germany), Mark (Portland, Oregon), Katie (Colorado), Zigor (Basque), and Marta (Poland). We walked together each day, went to the same restaurants and bars together in the evening, and slept in the same *albergue* at night. I was ready to move from such a personal, solitary journey to a more collective journey. Having each hiked our own Camino, it was about reaching the final destination together. It was decided that we'd lock arms and walk into the Cathedral Square as one.

For me, that feeling of all coming together is what felt the most spiritual. The long days of solitude on the Meseta were replaced by a tangible sense of community. It struck me deeply that I was a part of something so much bigger than me.

Transcending Time

On one of the last hilly days in Galicia, I had ascended a peak, and having reached the top, I again turned around to appreciate where I had come from. Behind me was a long, steady line of pilgrims coming up the hill from a field that stretched as far as I could see. I remember thinking, "Wow! I know God is everywhere, but I am certain God is here right now."

Something about that continuous flow of people in such a beautiful place is an image that will always stick with me. It is a picture of what humanity could be if we all came together and honored one another's journeys. In reflecting on the magic of those final days on the Camino, I think that one of the reasons the image of so many pilgrims coming up that path—marching toward Santiago together—struck me so profoundly is because it is a reflection of what it takes to effect cultural change, like advancing to the next generation of breast cancer screening for the good of all. It's going to take all of us, one by one, one right after the other, until we collectively "get there."

"When something becomes spiritual, for the collective good of all, it becomes a movement. When something becomes a movement, there's no ignoring it. And before you know it, the system has to change because of the spiritual force that is breaking it down and demanding it to be better."

In the final leg of the Camino, I not only got the feeling that I was united with those who were walking on the same path, but I also could not help but think about the millennia of history on the path beneath my feet—those millions of pilgrims who had gone before me. People have been making the pilgrimage to Santiago for more than a thousand years and will continue to do so long beyond the span of all of our lives. I understood that I was but a speck, a tiny dot, in that continuum.

In much the same way, I also came to peace with the idea that humanity was forging onward before I was born and will continue to do so once I am gone. As Ecclesiastes says, "There is a time for everything, and a season for every activity under the heavens…God has made everything beautiful in its time." All will be well no matter what, even for my family, just as it should be.

That reminded me to also appreciate all who have played such an important role in the detection of breast cancer and the care of breast cancer patients to date, as well as those whose lives have been lost to breast cancer and those families who have suffered the loss of a loved one. We've come a long way since the days when we lost 72,000 a year to breast cancer, but we can't forget about the 41,000 who died last year, who will die this year, and will continue to do so until something changes. With more advanced screening techniques like Molecular Breast Imaging and other new modalities, and better treatment protocols, we can move closer to reducing the number of deaths per year. The more we can come together, the sooner we will see this happen.

Some of the brightest minds in medicine and healthcare are revamping screening and moving closer to improved treatments and one day, a cure. We can all be thankful for that. We also have people in powerful political and economic positions who have good hearts and are dedicated to progress on breast cancer detection and treatments.

When enough people come together and walk in the same direction with a collective understanding of what is right and necessary for all, a spiritual energy—something that is indescribable and larger than life—begins to build. Something of a contagious spiritual wind begins to push everyone along, in the same direction, together, toward the same destination.

When something becomes spiritual, for the collective good of all, it becomes a movement. When something becomes a movement, there's no ignoring it. And before you know it, the system has to change because of the spiritual force that is breaking it down and demanding it to be better.

If your call isn't to hike the whole proverbial Camino, don't worry. You don't have to be a researcher or a scientist or fundraiser to make an impact. Simply tell a friend or family member about breast density.

Learn about the different kinds of screening and help others become more aware. Find out your own density, read your screening report, and push your doctor to help you get the breast cancer screening you deserve to have, and help a friend do the same. Do whatever is best for you while also considering the collective ramifications of our journey together as women. Play a part in where we're going, together, and maybe one day others will reflect on the path we paved.

- 12 -

Culmination

*"Blessed are those who persevere under trial, because when they
have stood the test, they will receive the crown of life that God has
promised to those who love him."*
-St. James

M any pilgrims skip the first two legs of the Camino and start
somewhere along the final leg, most in the town of Sarria,
sixty-two miles from Santiago. That's the closest point on the route that
one can begin the pilgrimage and still earn a certificate of completion,
called a *compostela*.

My husband and I had hiked about sixty miles total the year before,
when we were in the Galicia area celebrating our thirtieth anniversary.
On that trip, as intriguing as it was to join the other pilgrims on the
very last part of their walk into the Cathedral Square, I could also tell
that I was missing a whole element. The weight of the emotion some
people had that day after hiking as far as they had was palpable.

Honestly, I kind of felt like I was cheating. I could tell that even
though I was seeing the same cathedral as every other person who was
entering the Old Town Square, they had gone on an inner journey that
I had not. John and I had an opportunity to go to the Pilgrim's Mass
that day at the Cathedral, but we chose not to go because, well, we
weren't pilgrims. It just didn't feel right.

> *"The mental reframing, the emotional openings, and the spiritual revelations had all occurred because I left my usual world behind and created the space for something else. All because I had allowed myself to become a student of the Path."*

This time, however, was different. Only 10 percent of those who hike the Camino Frances traverse the whole five hundred miles, but once all those steps have been taken over a period of several weeks, a lasting perspective change has surely occurred. Having endured the physical leg through the Pyrenees, the mental leg through the Meseta, and the spiritual segment through Galicia, I naturally began to reflect about not only my entire Camino journey and its challenges, but on the inner journey as well.

All the insightful lessons I had learned on the path.

All the mental reframing, the emotional openings, and the spiritual revelations that had occurred because I left my usual world behind and created the space for something else.

All because I had allowed myself to become a student of the Path.

As I mentioned earlier, I had no planned schedule whatsoever upon stepping foot on the Camino back in Saint-Jean-Pied-de-Port. After three days in the Pyrenees, I had stayed in Pamplona for a day to recover, spent an extra day in Burgos, and then paused for three days in Leon for the blood test. I had booked my return flight with plenty of time to spare so that I was not rushed. I was determined to just let things unfold however they were supposed to unfold.

In the final stretch, just two miles outside of Santiago, I was relaxing with my Camino family after our last long days walk when Katharina turned to me and asked, "Did you know that tomorrow, when we walk into the Cathedral Square, it will be our fortieth day?"

"Really?" I said. I was a little surprised by the symbolism of the number forty, a number that has a lot of biblical significance. I had no idea we'd be finishing the Camino on our fortieth day, and I certainly had not specifically planned it that way. Many theologians assert that Jesus went out into the desert for forty days to awaken his purpose and become who he was supposed to become in order to begin his ministry.

The Camino is a metaphorical desert, as I am sure it is meant to be. It's off the grid, away from societal norms, and removed from culture.

It's where lessons are learned and personal development is bound to take place. I certainly felt over those forty days that I had made "friends" with my cancer, made peace with whatever was to come, and was concretely firm in my path forward to push, alongside many other forces, for the next generation of breast cancer screening. I would not be quieted. I would not be deterred. I would persevere. I had stepped into that arena, and I would stay there. I had come a long way, and there was no turning back now.

The Final Stretch

Forty days earlier, I didn't know if I would make it, how long it would take me, or how much money I would raise. I had no way of comprehending the scope of the physical or inner journey I was about to embark on. Finding myself now just steps away from the end of what I had been journeying toward for weeks was mind-boggling and emotionally complex.

The final kilometer of the Way walks pilgrims up a hill that overlooks the city where the three tall spires of the Cathedral tower above its surroundings, a glimpse of the final destination just before it is reached. The path then winds down right into the heart of the city, heading straight for the Cathedral. The emotional gravity in the air is heavy as pilgrims walk their last half kilometer. Most people are walking at a moderate pace with their heads down, pensive and quiet. There is very little light-hearted or frivolous conversation.

Just before we entered the Square, Katharina, Mark, Zigor, Marta, Katie, and I locked arms, as we had planned. We then walked into the Square together. A bagpiper serenaded us as we entered. Suddenly, we were right in the middle of the Old Town Square, right in front of the towering 330-foot-tall Santiago de Compostela Cathedral, with its gothic towers and intricate art and statues. Pilgrims have all kinds of visceral reactions to having completed their journey. Some were on their knees, kissing the cobblestone of the Square. Others were sobbing. Others had their hands in the air, praising God and giving thanks. We all shed a few tears as we walked in.

As we made it to the center of the Square, we hugged, took pictures, laughed, cried, and sometimes did all these things at once. As Katie put it, "This is the happiest worst day of my life." Or maybe it was the "worst happiest" day of our lives. I say that because of how emotionally complex it was. A certain wordlessness comes at this particular moment. Consequently, most pilgrims do not fully verbally express what they are experiencing.

To be sure, I found myself unusually quiet as well. The competing emotions of happiness to have made it and sadness in being done, plus relief, uneasiness, and calmness combined with a touch of anxiety, leave one without words to describe the fullness of the experience. Fortunately, like most other pilgrims, I did not feel the need to express it. Rather, I chose to simply feel the deep gratitude that comes with having experienced something that is not completely explainable, something of which words are not entirely worthy.

I had walked in alongside my Camino family, but then my mind drifted back to my own personal journey. I felt so grateful to still be physically able to walk five hundred miles, for the love I felt for the Camino Family I had just met, for the family back at home who loved me, for everyone who had donated to Density MATTERS, and for Camino itself, for showing me the Way.

Seeing "It" Swing

Several days before reaching Santiago, there begins a lot of talk up and down the trail about whether "it" or the "thing" will swing or not when we get there—the "it" and the "thing" being a giant silver thurible called the Botafumeiro, which is Galician for "smoke expeller."

It weighs about 175 pounds and is about five feet tall—making it one of the largest thuribles in the world—and is suspended on a pulley system from the top of the cathedral ceiling. It is loaded with incense, lit on fire, and set into motion by monks pulling on the thick ropes of the pulley; swinging it back and forth in front of the main altar, so high that it almost touches the ceiling on both sides.

Centuries ago, legend has it that this was done at every service to purify tired and unbathed pilgrims who at that time stayed in the lofts of the Cathedral. In modern times, the meaning of the ceremonial swinging has changed to being more of a blessing to pilgrims as they complete their pilgrimages and go forth to whatever is next in their lives. Unfortunately, now it "swings" only on high holidays, or when someone donates around 400 euros, hence the angst about whether pilgrims will get to see it swing, or not.

There was a very strong rumor that the thurible was going to swing the evening of our arrival into Santiago, so I had planned to settle into the little apartment that Katharina and I had rented for a couple days and attend the Pilgrim's Mass then. Most pilgrims attend the Mass whether or not they are spiritual or religious. Not only does it take place in one of the greatest architectural masterpieces in Spain, but who knows, you might get to see the Botafumeiro swing. To be certain, the Camino journey itself *is* the reward, but it really is an extra bonus if you get to see it swing.

After an hour or so in the Cathedral Square taking pictures and soaking in the unique atmosphere, we were all contemplating what would come next and feeling a little unsettled each in our own way. A Mass was to be held in about half an hour, and at that point, we all felt drawn to it.

What a blessing that turned out to be. Although we were not expecting to see the Botafumeiro swing, the Mass was truly moving that day as we stood in the back, near the entrance. We drank in the music, the ancient architecture, the baroque art, and the feeling of timelessness, knowing that pilgrims from centuries before us had stood where we were now standing.

The entire service was in Spanish, so I couldn't understand most of it. But still, I found myself, once again, getting quite emotional being in that place. I reflected on the journey and the many gifts The Way of Saint James had bestowed on many souls before and will do so for many after me.

The beautiful Mass ended, and we slowly and reluctantly made our way toward the exit. From the corner of my eye, I saw activity near the altar. Out came monks in dark scarlet robes, adding incense, lighting the thurible, and preparing to set the Botafumeiro in motion. We would, in fact, get to see it swing!

Priests in green robes crowded around the thurible to pray over the Botafumeiro and bless the pilgrims. The thurible started smoking, the priests walked away, and one monk gave it a slight shove to set in motion. Then a handful of monks controlling the pulley began yanking it every few seconds to help the thurible gain momentum. Swinging slowly at first, the Botafumeiro began flying back and forth over pilgrims' heads within a minute, painting the length of the church with heavy smoke. For me, it was the perfect culmination of my time on the Camino. After forty transformative days, I felt like the Botafumeiro was sending me off into the world and blessing my journey. It felt like a personal benediction.

Take everything that you've learned on The Path and, like Saint James, use your voice to bring justice and equality—through your love—into the spaces in this world that ignite your heart.

Keep Walking, Trusting, and Loving

The next day, I found myself wandering down to the Cathedral Square, where all Camino pilgrims complete their journeys, just to watch them have the same experience that had been so moving for me the day before. I sat there by myself for quite a while, watching pilgrims parade into the Square from the path: young and old, limping and almost running, bedraggled and refreshed, dirty and clean, arm in arm or hand in hand with others, or alone in tears.

No two pilgrims were alike, just as no two outer or inner journeys are ever alike. No matter the age, race, gender, or nationality of the person, the dominant energy in the Square was joy. Deep-seated, divine joy filled that space. And it brought me joy, too, to see other people also accomplish something that they had worked so hard for.

"You don't have to be an expert. You don't have to have it all figured out. You don't have to meet all your expectations or worry about the expectations of others. You just have to be willing. Willing to learn. Willing to fail. Willing to venture out into the unknown and take one step after another as you move through the wilderness."

I also found myself thinking about the Botafumeiro the day before and how, although I was so fortunate to get to see the Botafumeiro swing, there were so many other areas in life where we are yet to see the fruits of our efforts…where we are yet to see it swing…where the culmination of our efforts is yet to be realized, like getting women access to the best breast cancer screening and technology they deserve. As moving as it was to watch people walk into the Cathedral Square and see them reach the crowning achievement of their Camino journey, it also fanned the flame of determination within me to keep journeying and pushing forward toward my other goals.

My encouragement to you is to keep trusting whatever is on your heart. I am no one special. I had little hiking experience, no fundraising experience, and was brand new to the fields of breast cancer screening and cancer research. All I had were willing legs, an eager heart, and a mind that was hungry to learn. That's it.

Keep going out into the arena, whether things are aligning or not. You don't have to be an expert. You don't have to have it all figured out. You don't have to meet all your expectations or worry about the expectations of others. You just have to be willing. Willing to learn. Willing to fail. Willing to venture out into the unknown and take one step after another as you move through the wilderness. Willing to be seen in the arena as you pursue whatever it is you were made to do. When you're willing, you never know what might happen.

I hope you get to fulfill the dreams that are in your heart. I hope you see the fruits of your efforts. I hope your passions are validated. I hope you get to experience something that leaves you speechless and renews your spirit. I hope you contribute something with your life that moves us all forward, together, down the path, into a space of healing and unity. I hope you have the courage to unleash whatever is on your heart, as well as come alongside others and help them unleash whatever is on theirs. I hope you have the courage to walk your own path, even if it's lonely, even if it's scary, as well as empower others as they walk theirs. I hope you never stop entering the arena. The world needs your unique heart, mind, passion, and determination to help humankind heal, move forward, and flourish.

And when all is said and done, I hope you get to see "it" swing.

Acknowledgments

First, my deepest gratitude to those who were with me during the several long weeks of my diagnosis back in October and November of 2017: John (my husband of course!), Fr. Jesse, Wes and Ann, Sharon, Rayanne, Laura, and Paul. It was confusing with a lot of ups and downs—thank you for being there for me. You are the best.

Also, thanks to my husband, John, my kids, Evan, Julia, and Megan, as well as my Mom, Barbara, and brother, Kent, for giving me the space, time, and freedom to walk the Camino on my own terms. It was an experience of a lifetime, and I hope you each get to take the journey some time as well.

Giant hugs to my immediate and extended Camino family: Katharina, Mark, Marta, Katie, Zigor, Suzanne and Mike, Elizna and Hannah, Amanda, Shannon, Jane, Amanda, The Biloxi Boys, Jes, Jenn and Jodi, Lorna, Norm and Tony, Shelly, Dereatha and Larry, Barry and Dave, and to the many more who touched my life during my forty-day pilgrimage. I sincerely wish that our paths will cross again someday. I will remember you fondly for the rest of my days.

A special appreciation goes to the clergy of St. Michael's Episcopal Church: Jesse, Lisa, Al, Betsy, Laurie, and Judy, as well as to the entire congregation for your loving prayers, both then and always. I feel it! You are a special group of people.

Thanks a million to Kim, my friend and website designer, to Julia, for helping with my website and social media blogs/postings, and to Jeanne, for helping me spread my message locally and beyond. I couldn't have done it without you all!

And finally, a special thank you to Bob Lee, founder of Ride for 3 Reasons, and to Vince Foglia of the Foglia Family Foundation for making the fundraising for the Density MATTERS study all that it was. I am also very grateful for each and every donation, no matter how large or small. It just goes to show you that together, we can make a difference!

About the Author

Leslie Ferris Yerger was born and raised in Worthington, Indiana. She attended Purdue University, where she earned degrees in computer science and industrial management and was a member of the Sigma Kappa Sorority. She also obtained her masters degree in business administration (MBA) from the University of North Carolina at Chapel Hill. She is both a proud Boilermaker and Tar Heel.

Leslie was diagnosed with Stage 4 lobular breast cancer in November 2017, when abnormalities were found during a routine bone density scan. Unfortunately, her cancer was not visible on either a mammogram or a ultrasound, as is sometimes the case with lobular cancer hiding in dense breast tissue. This is not a failure of anyone, but it is simply a failure of our current technology. And now, along with all of her current work, Leslie seeks to make a positive impact in advancing the next major breakthrough in breast cancer screening, so more women with breast cancer become survivors. Fundraising during her Camino de Santiago walk in the fall of 2018 became her first means to that end.

Leslie lives in Hawthorn Woods, Illinois with her husband, John, and is the proud mother of their three children: Evan, Julia, and Megan. Leslie speaks at churches, women's and business groups, as well as not-for-profit organizations in order to educate the public about breast density and empower women to advocate for their own optimal screening. You may contact her at Leslie@walkthewaywithher.com.